This children's coloring book pays homage to the wonder of creation and the joy of life. I thank God for the inspiration that permeates each page and for guiding our paths with the light of love.

To my beloved family, whose support and affection are the colors that fill my life, I dedicate this work. May every line on these pages reflect the beauty of the moments we share together.

May this book be a constant reminder of gratitude and love, representing the heavenly union and earthly bonds that make our journey more colorful.

Hellen Santos
2024

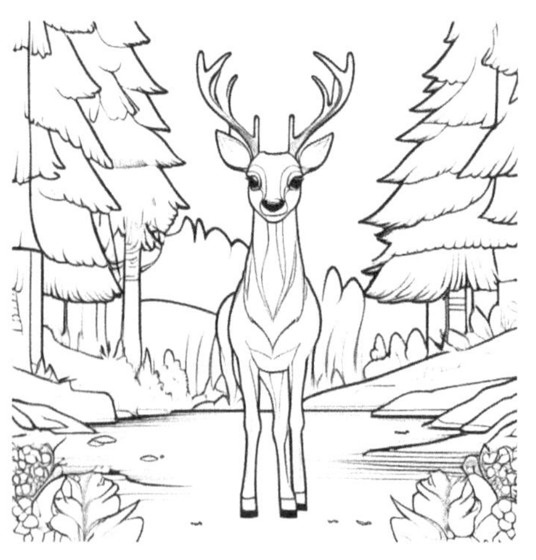
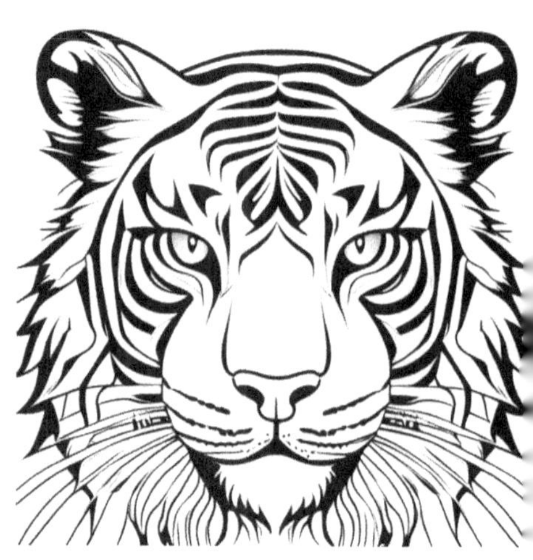

This Book Belongs to:

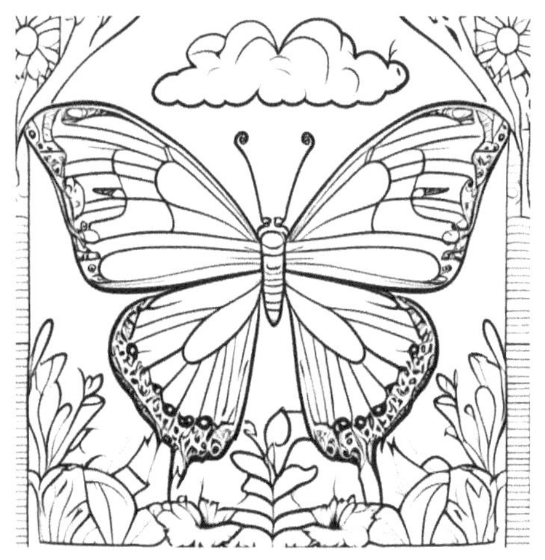
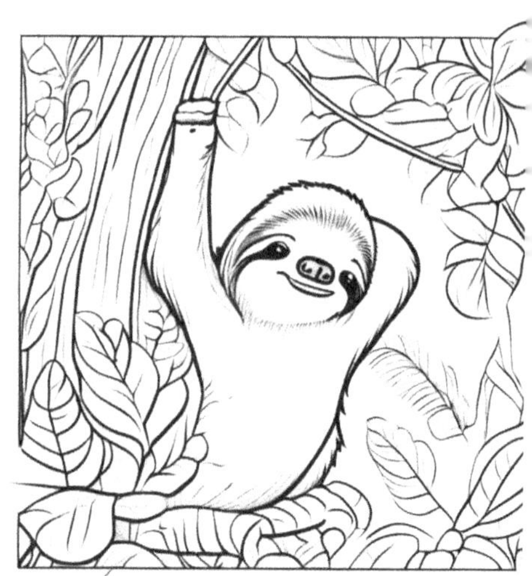

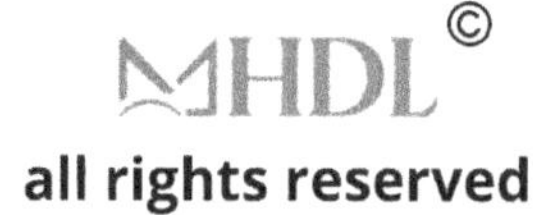

ALL RIGHTS RESERVED ©
2023

No part of this publication may be reproduced, distributed, or transmitted in any form or by any means, including photocopying, recording, or other electronic or mechanical methods, without the prior written permission of the publisher, except for brief quotations incorporated in critical reviews and other specific noncommercial uses. Any unauthorized replica of this work is prohibited.

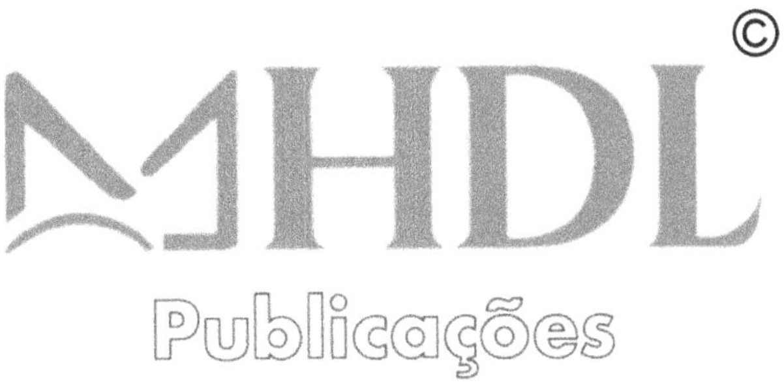

Test Color Page

North America:

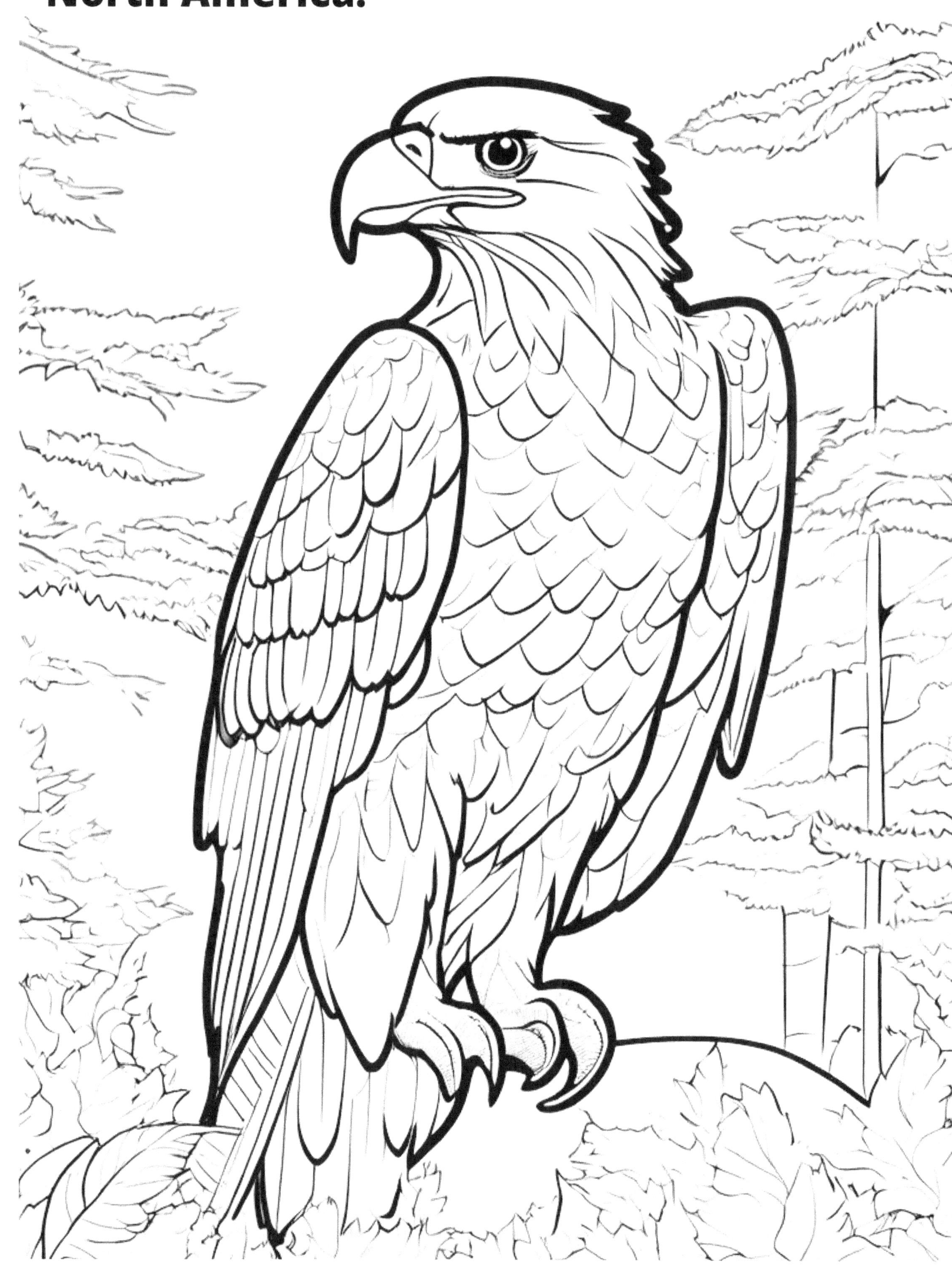

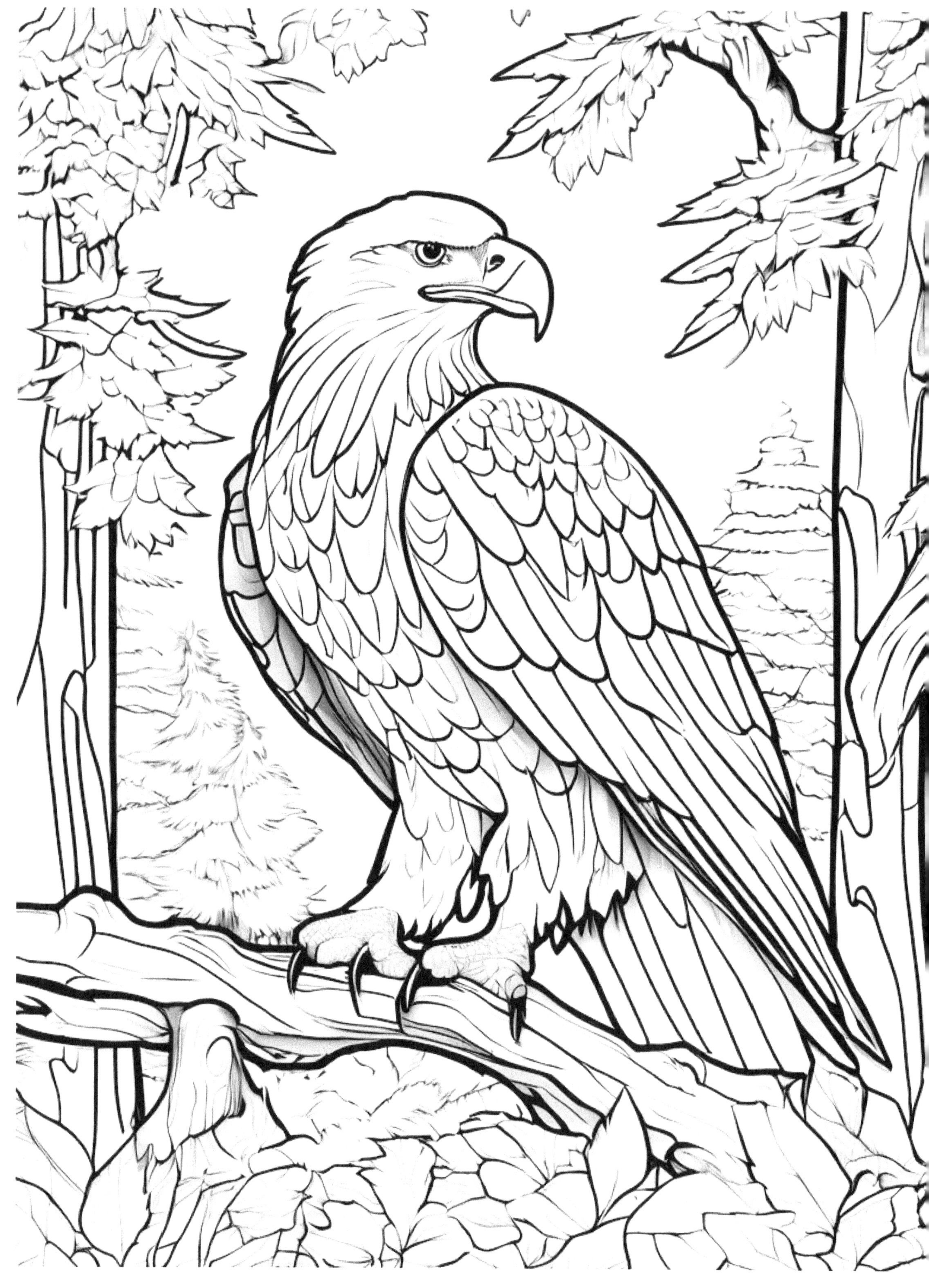

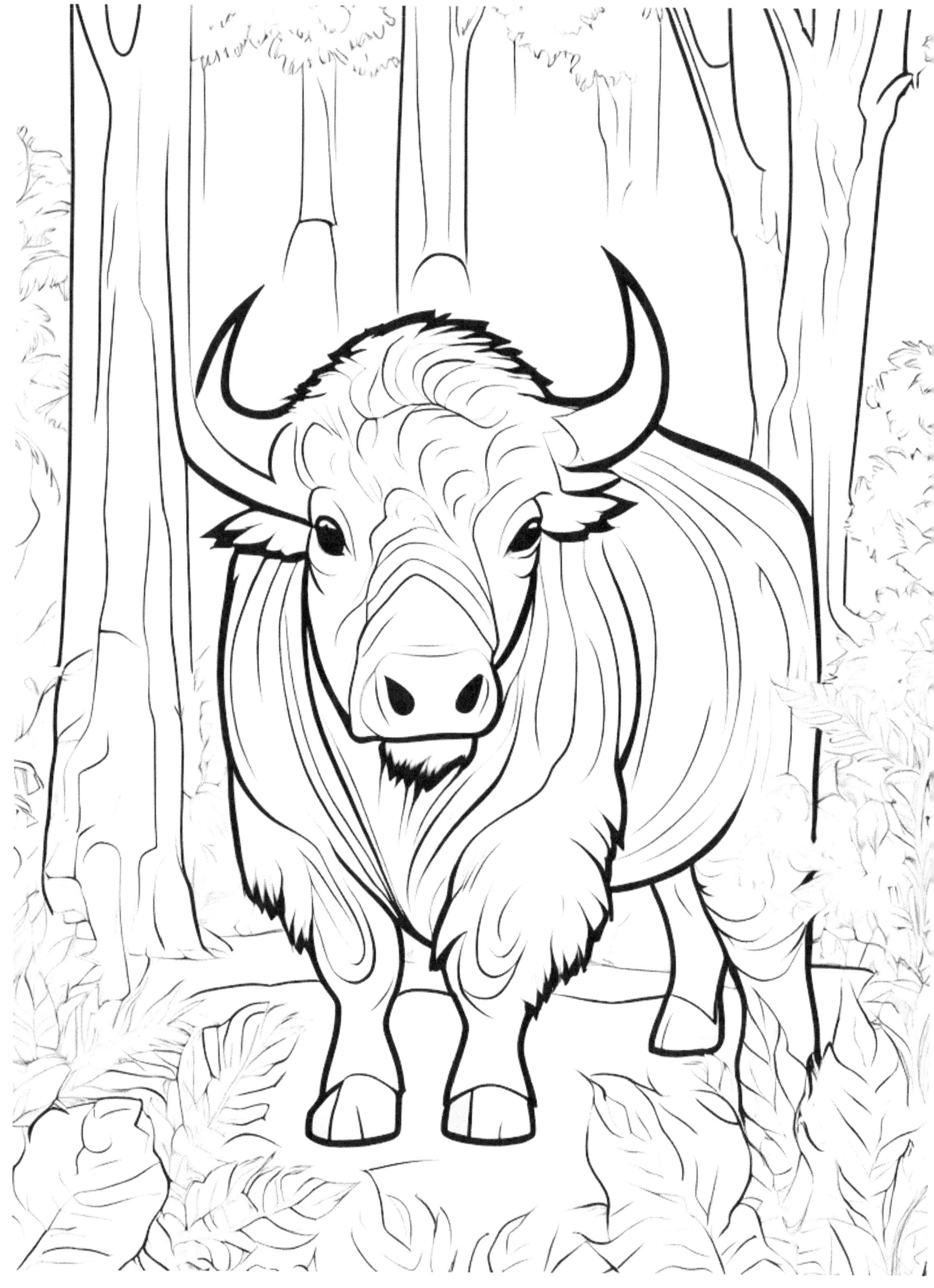

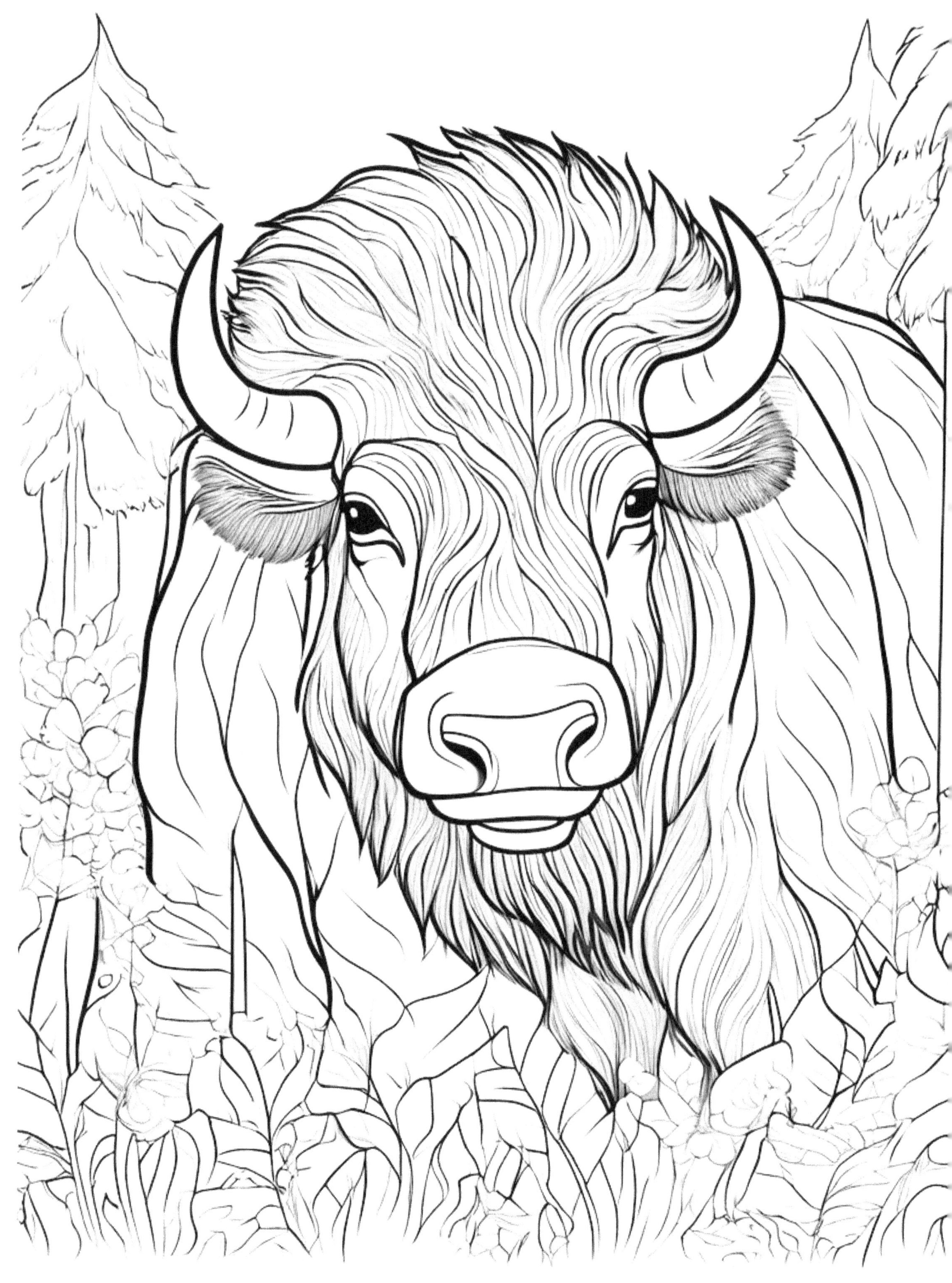

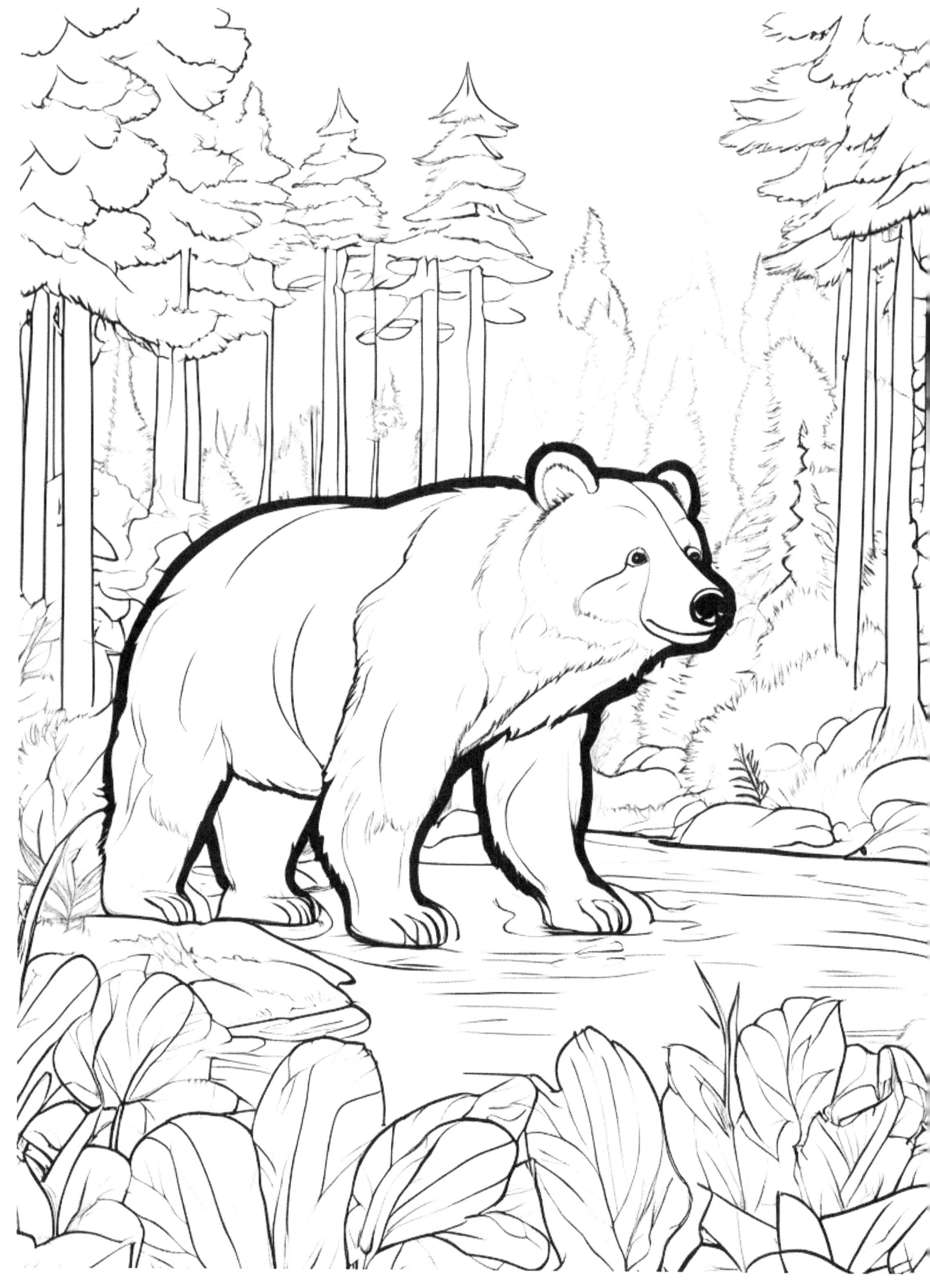

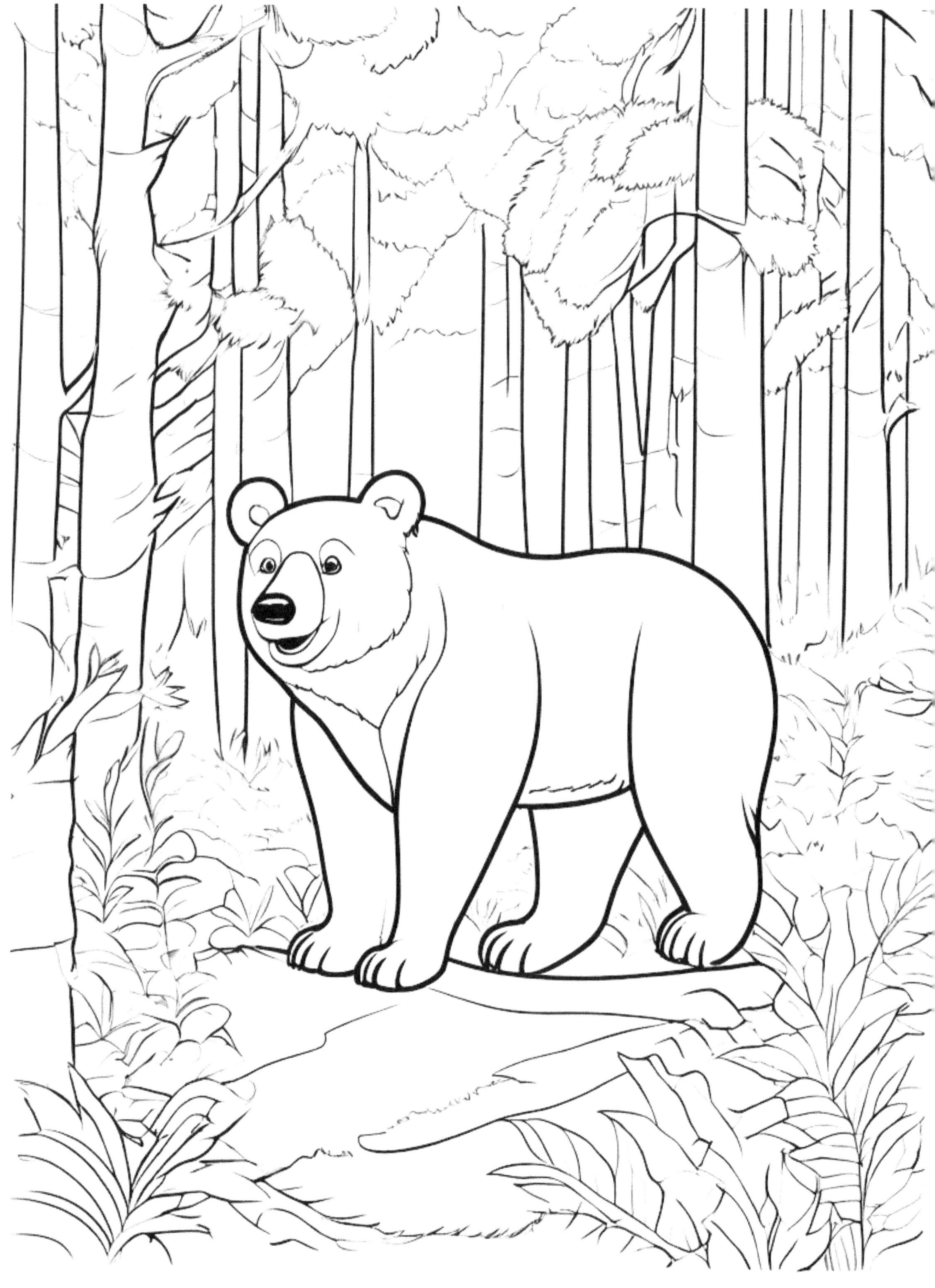

Africa:

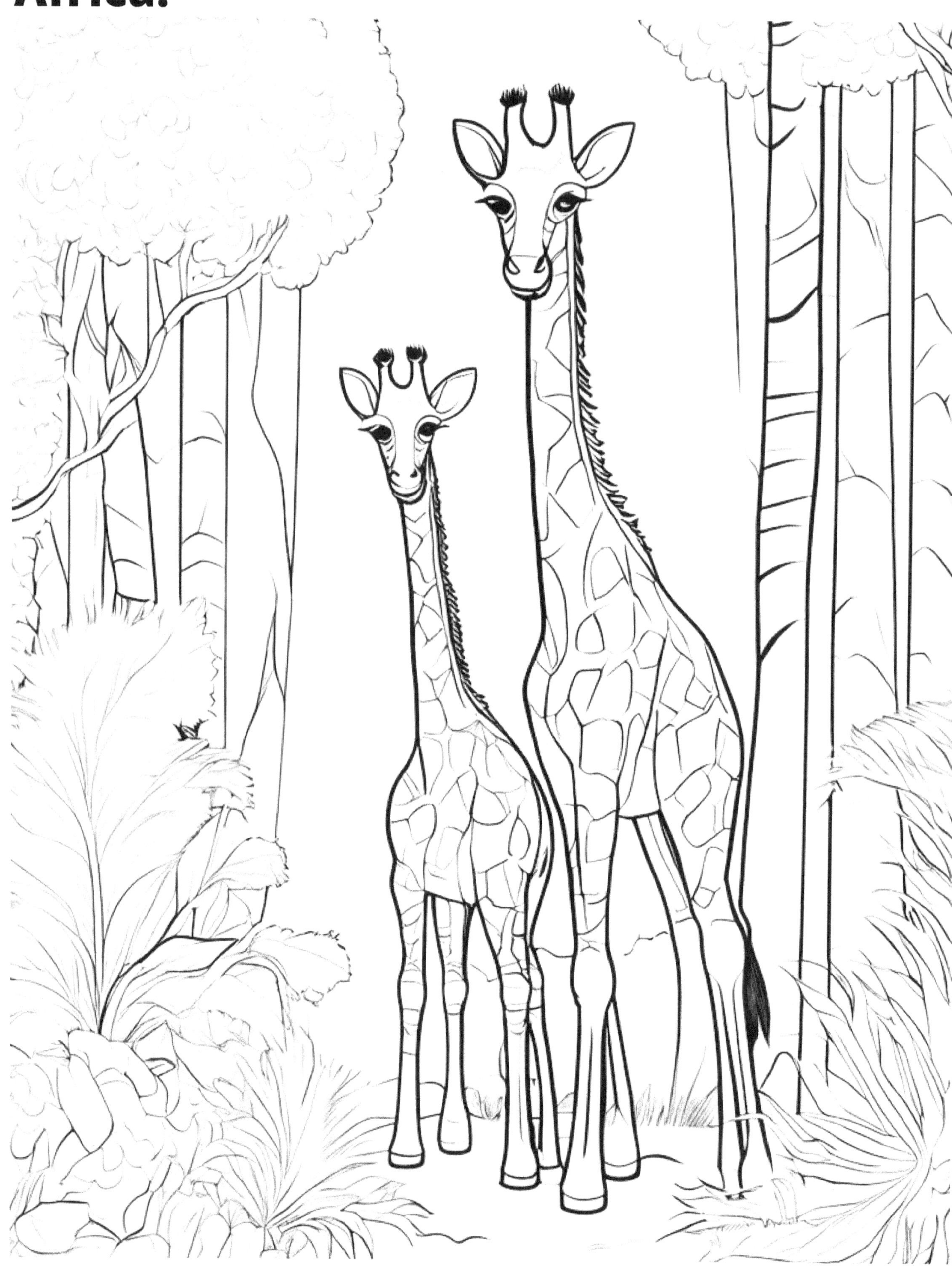

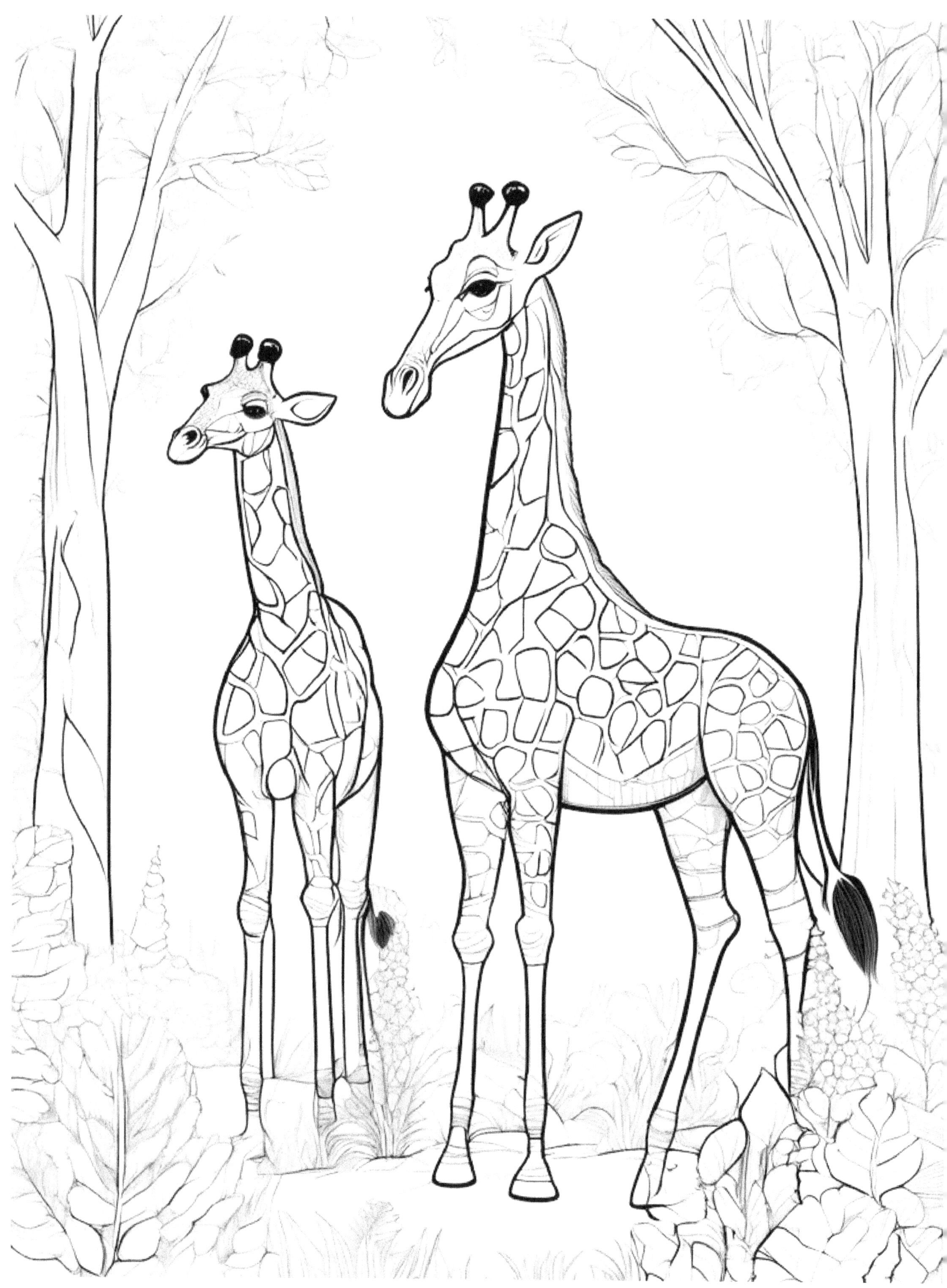

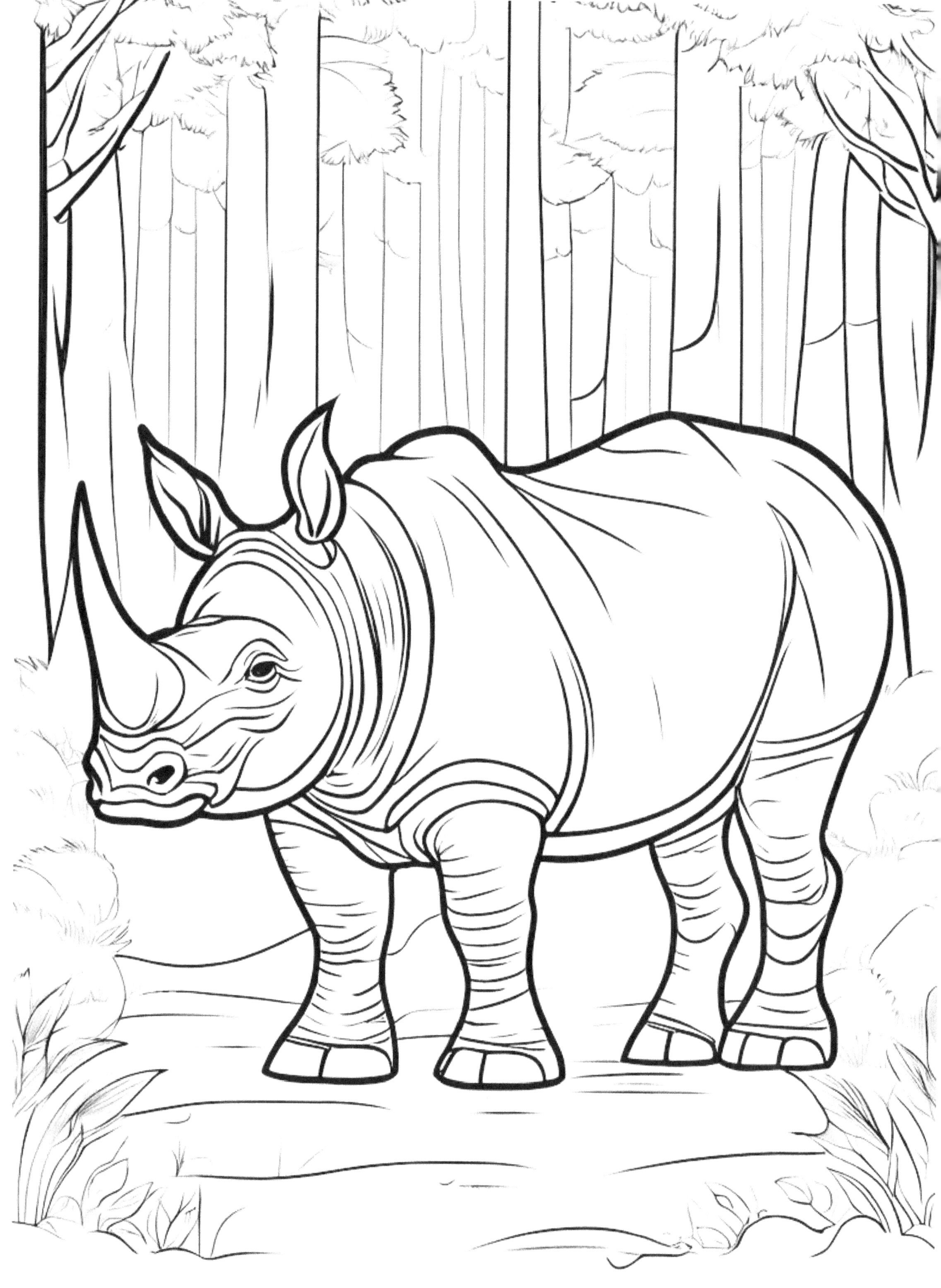

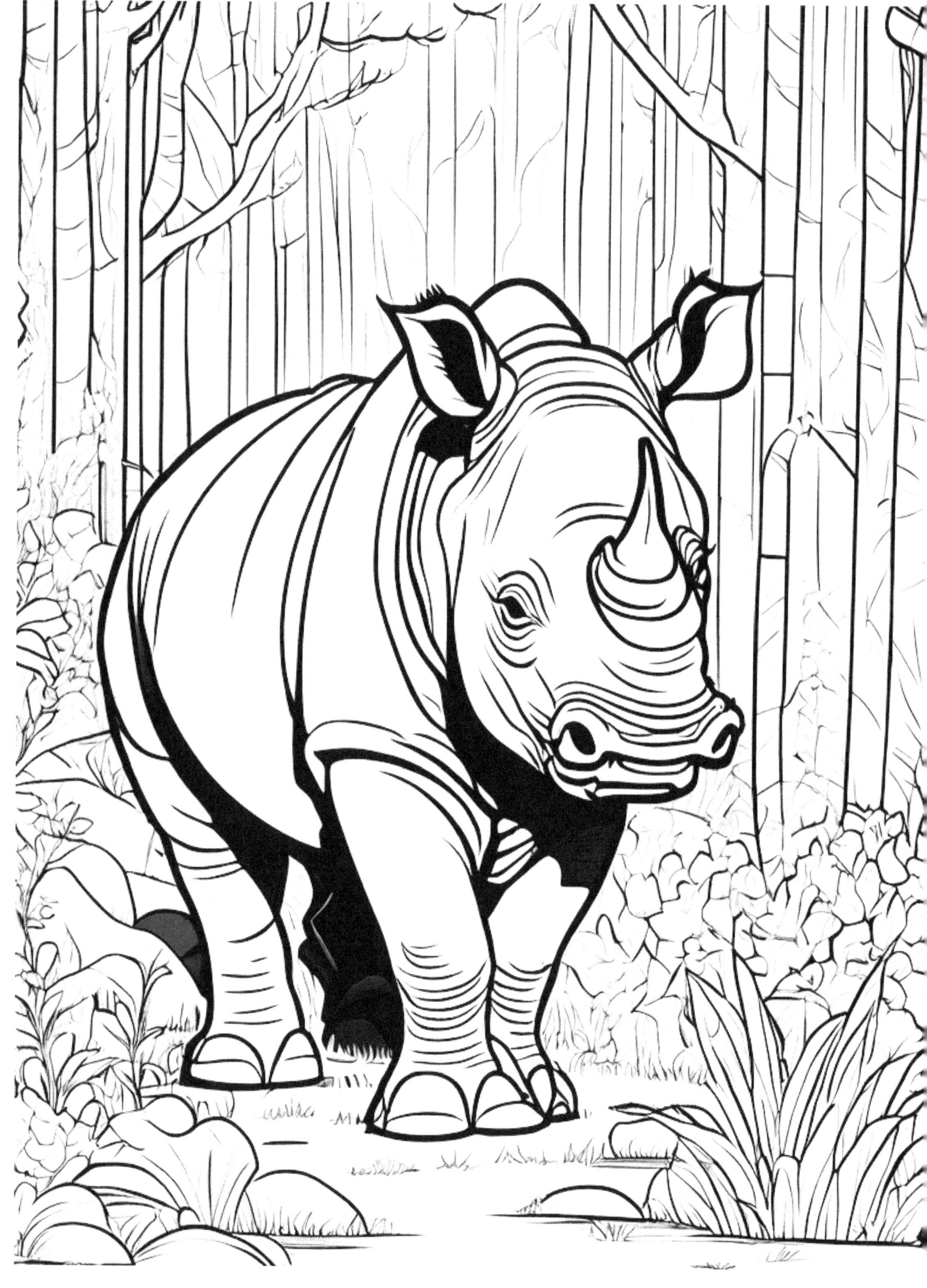

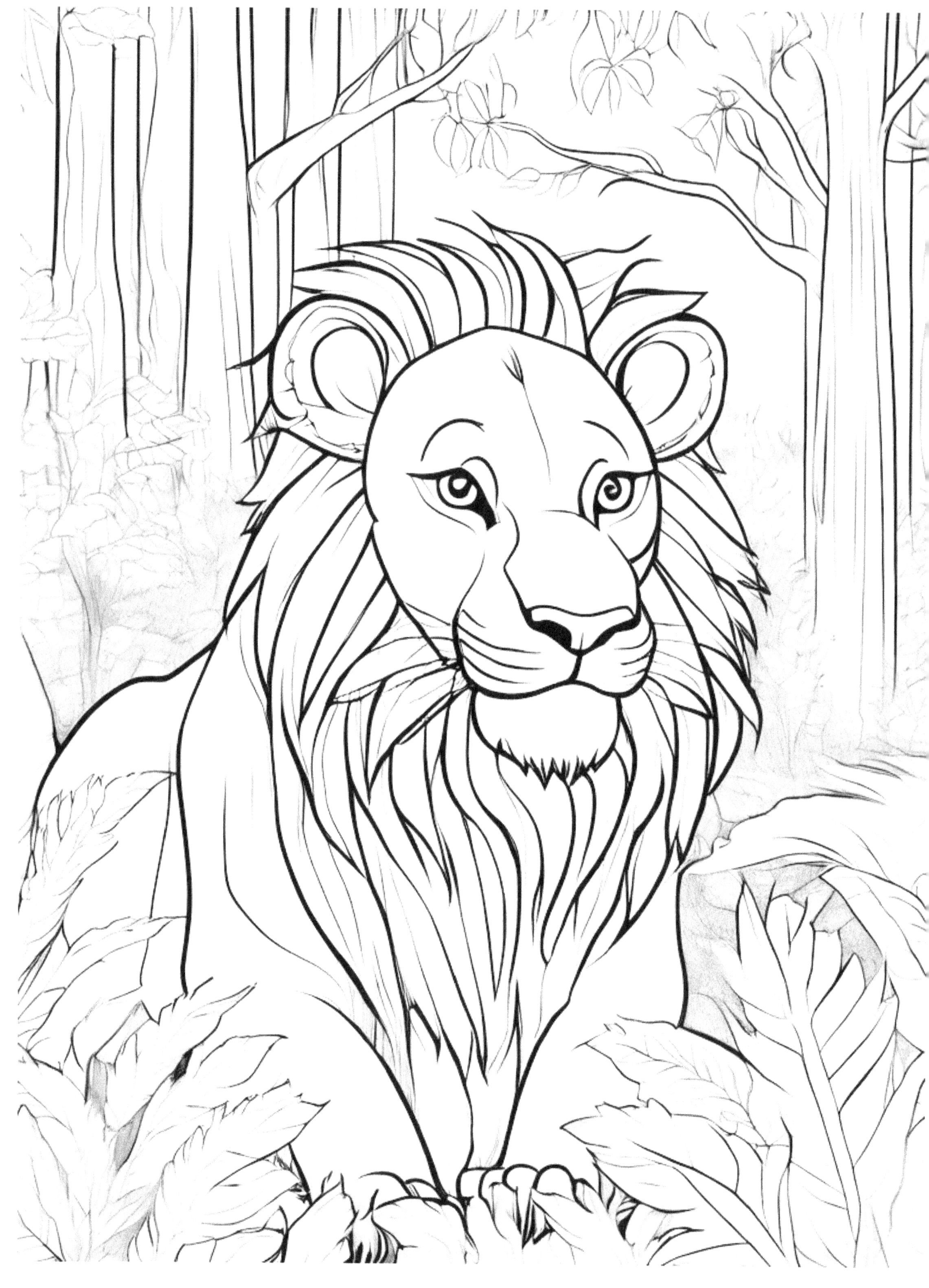

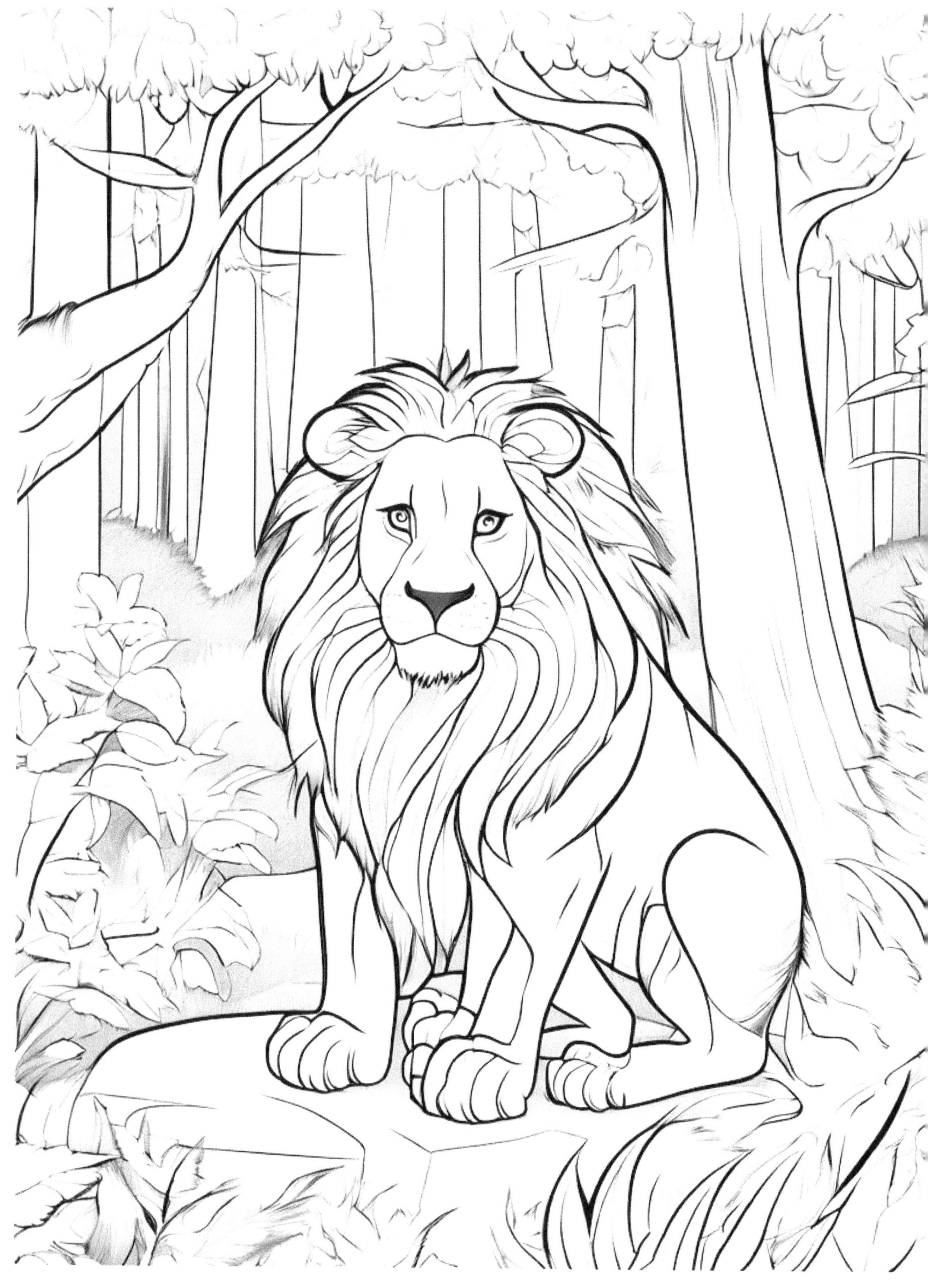

South America:

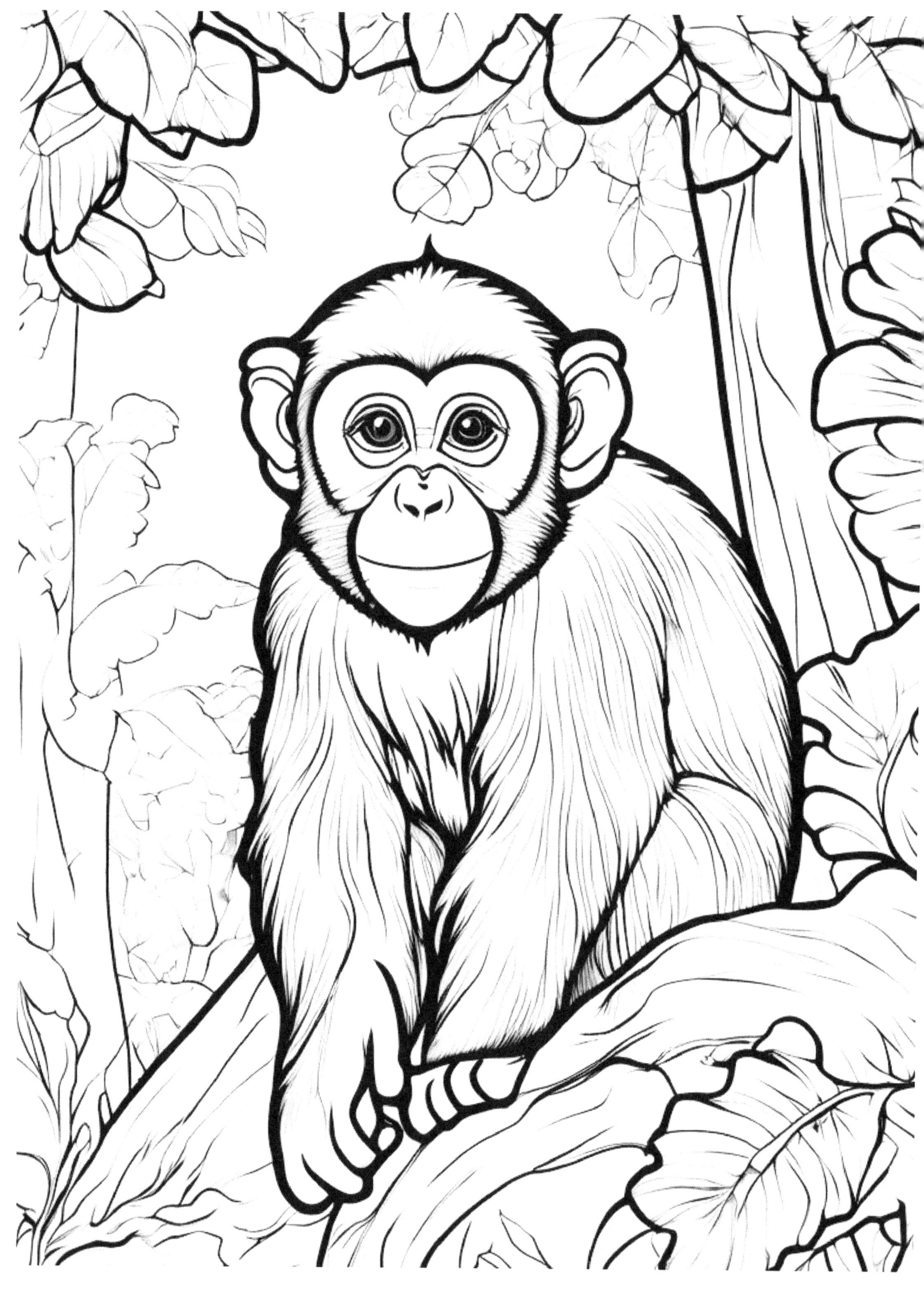

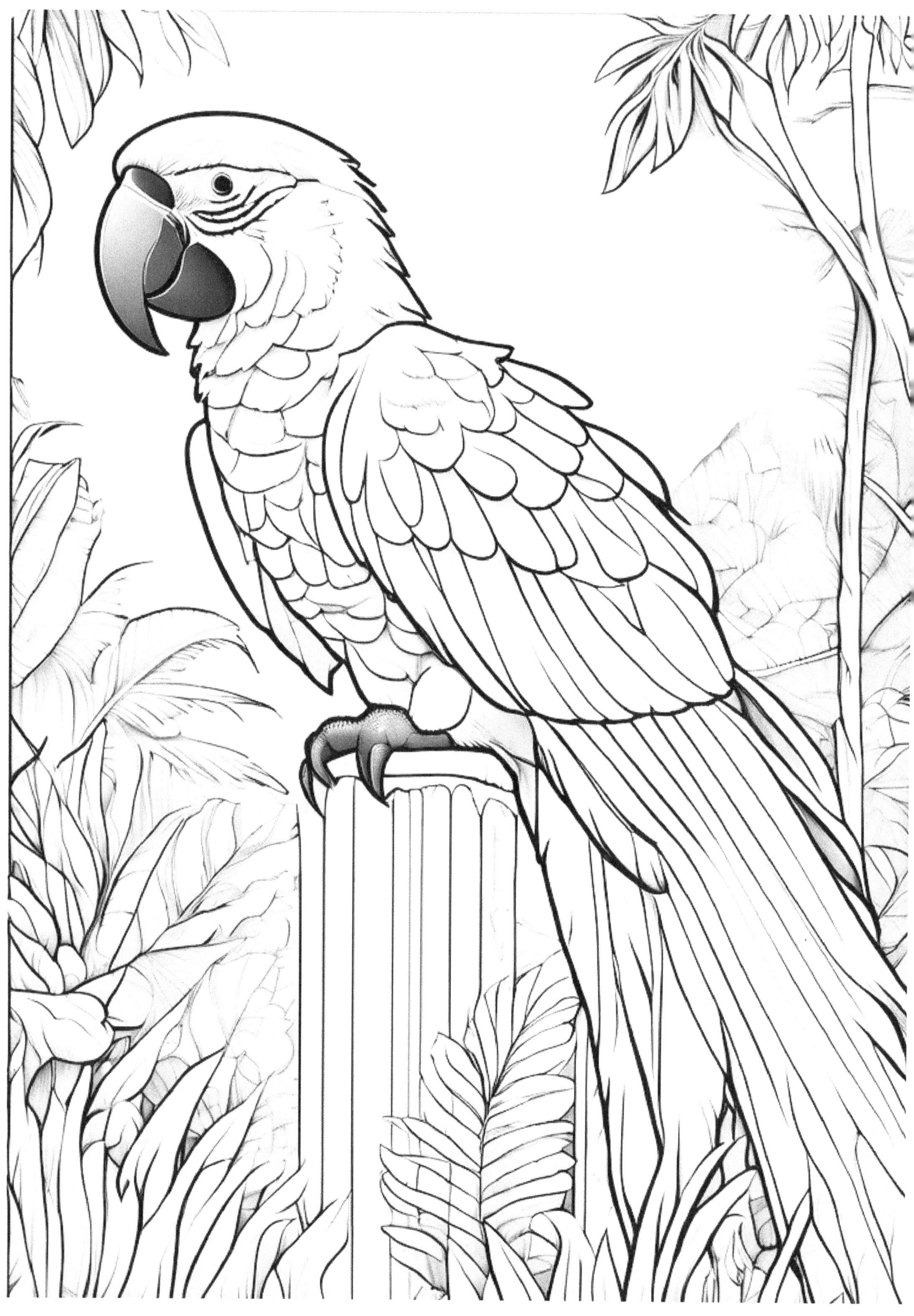

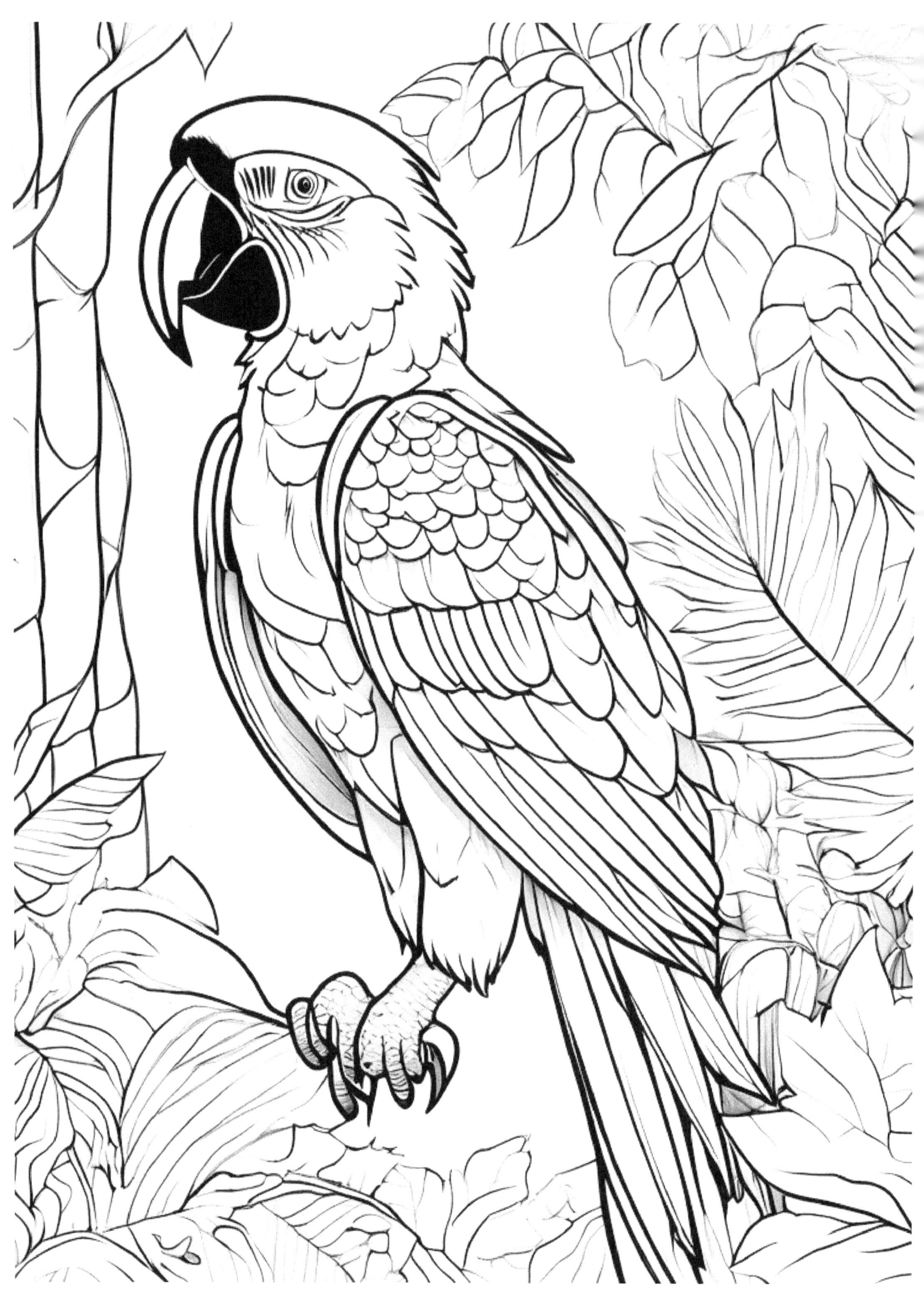

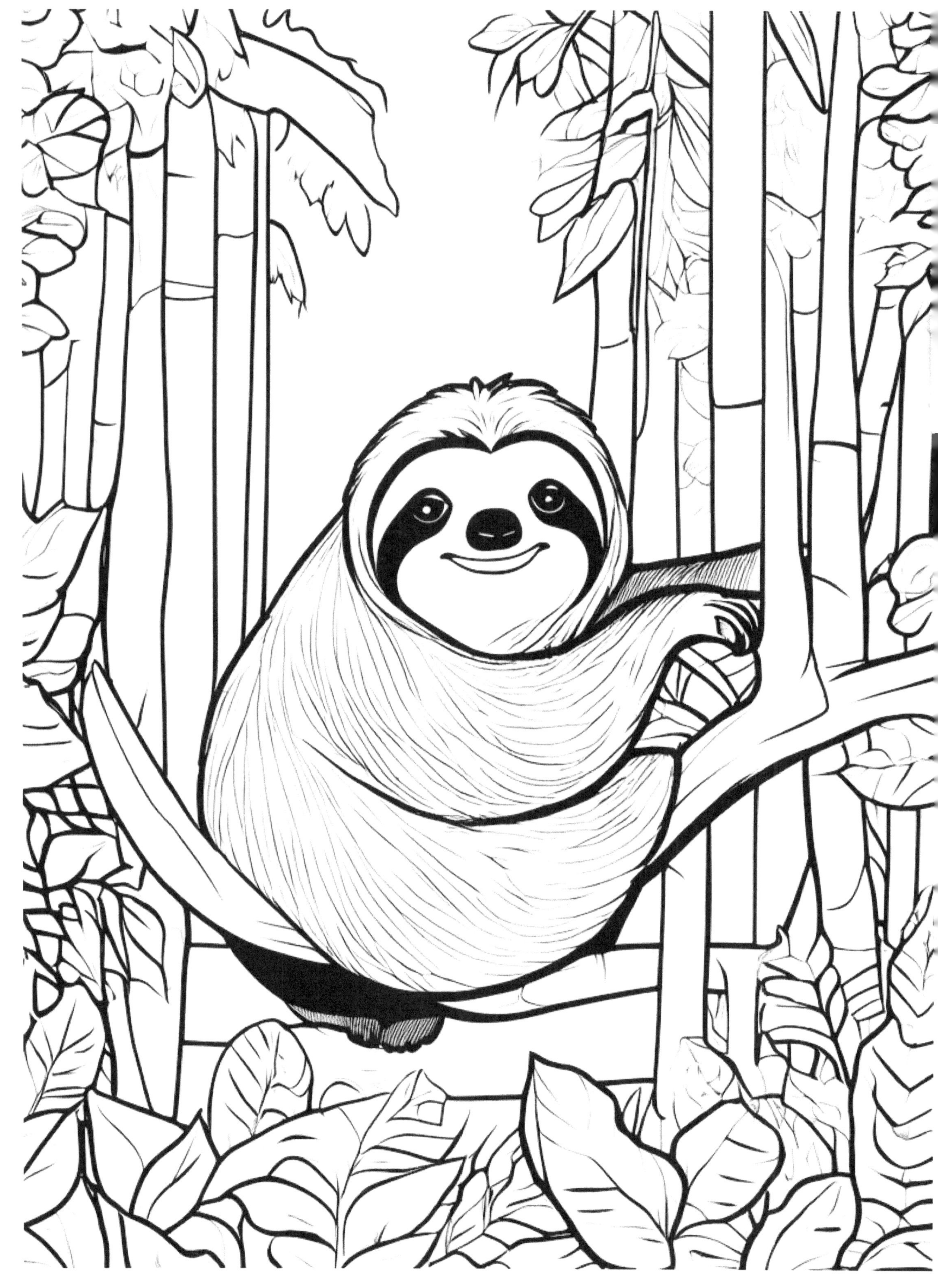

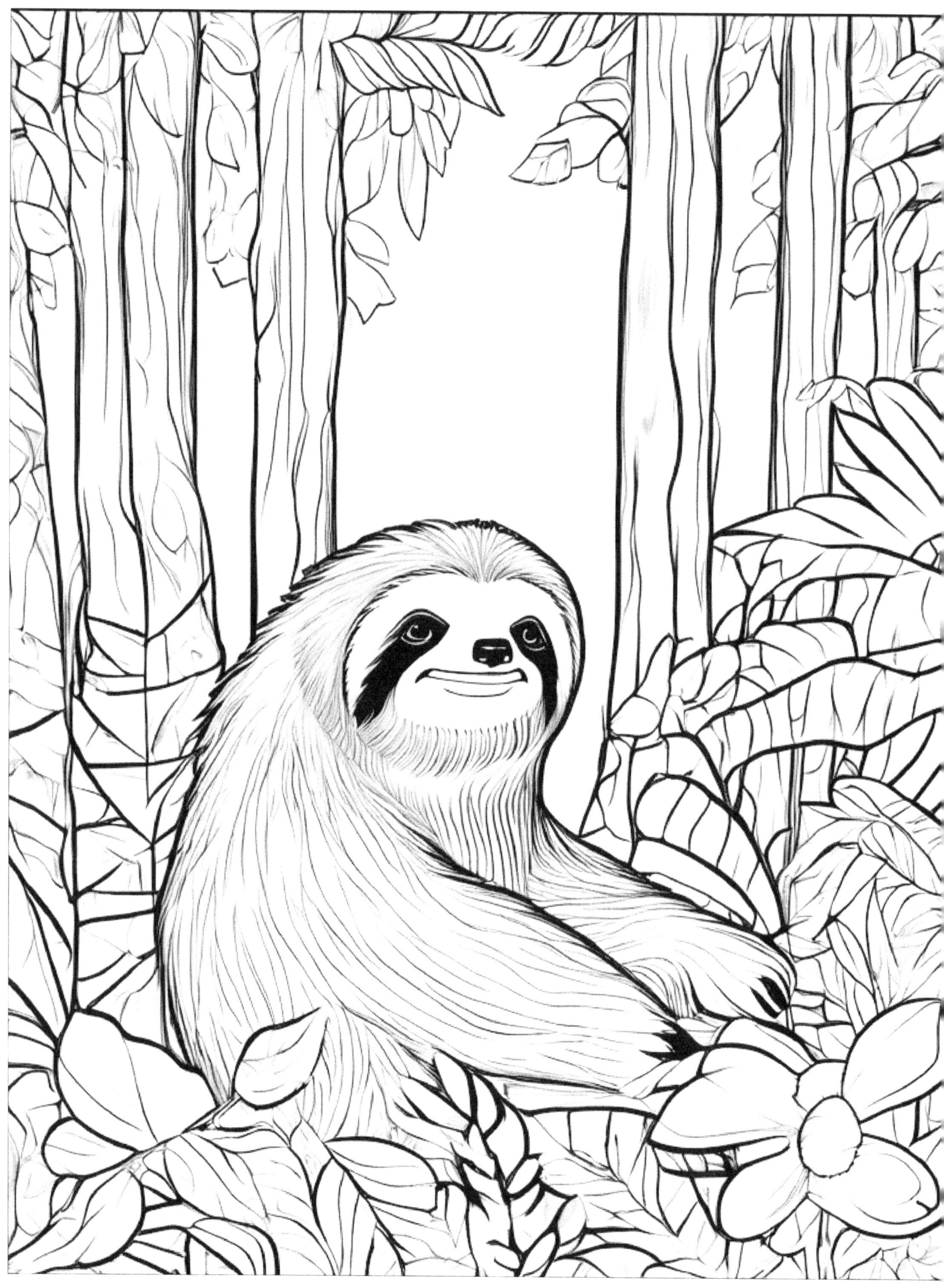

Asia:

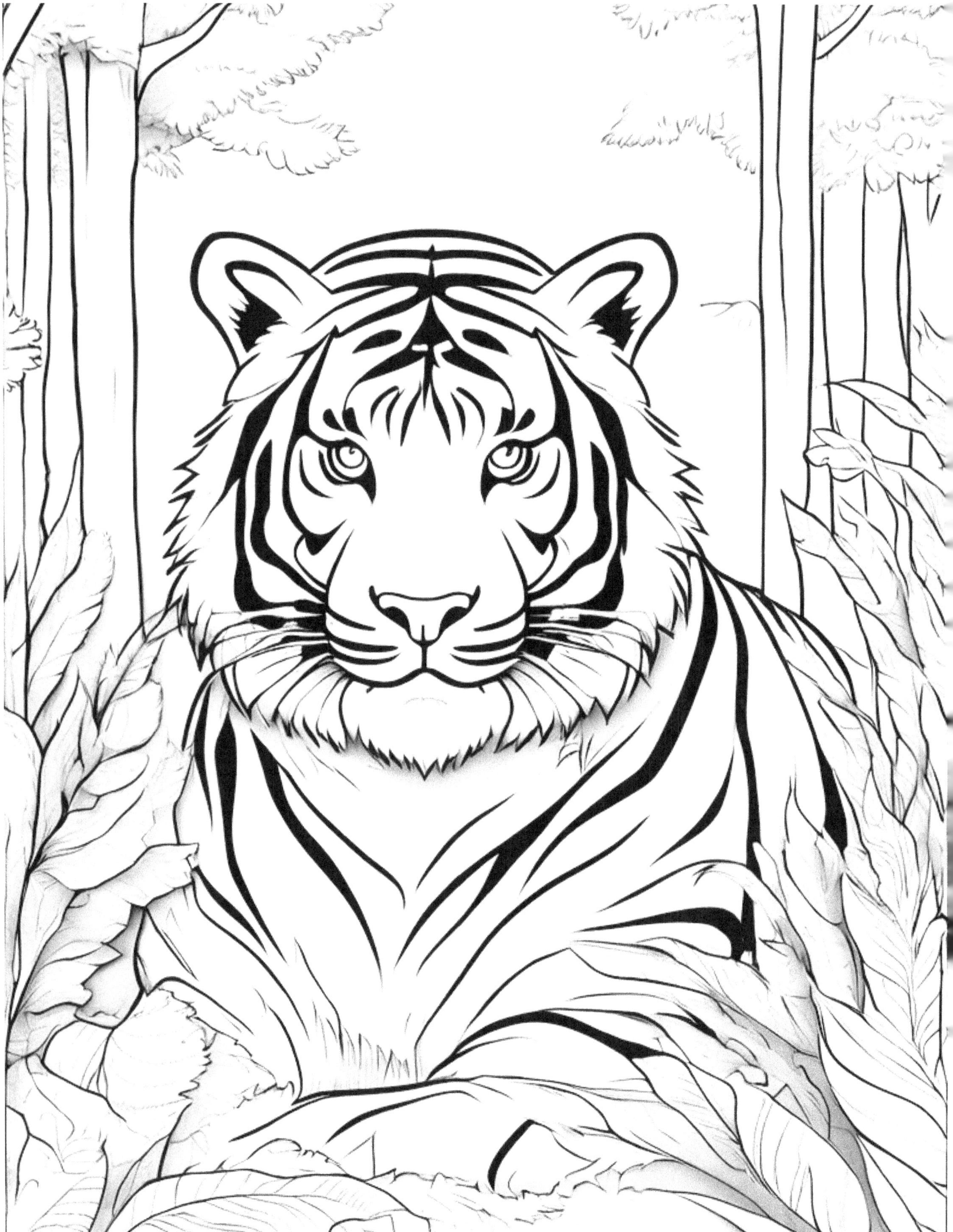

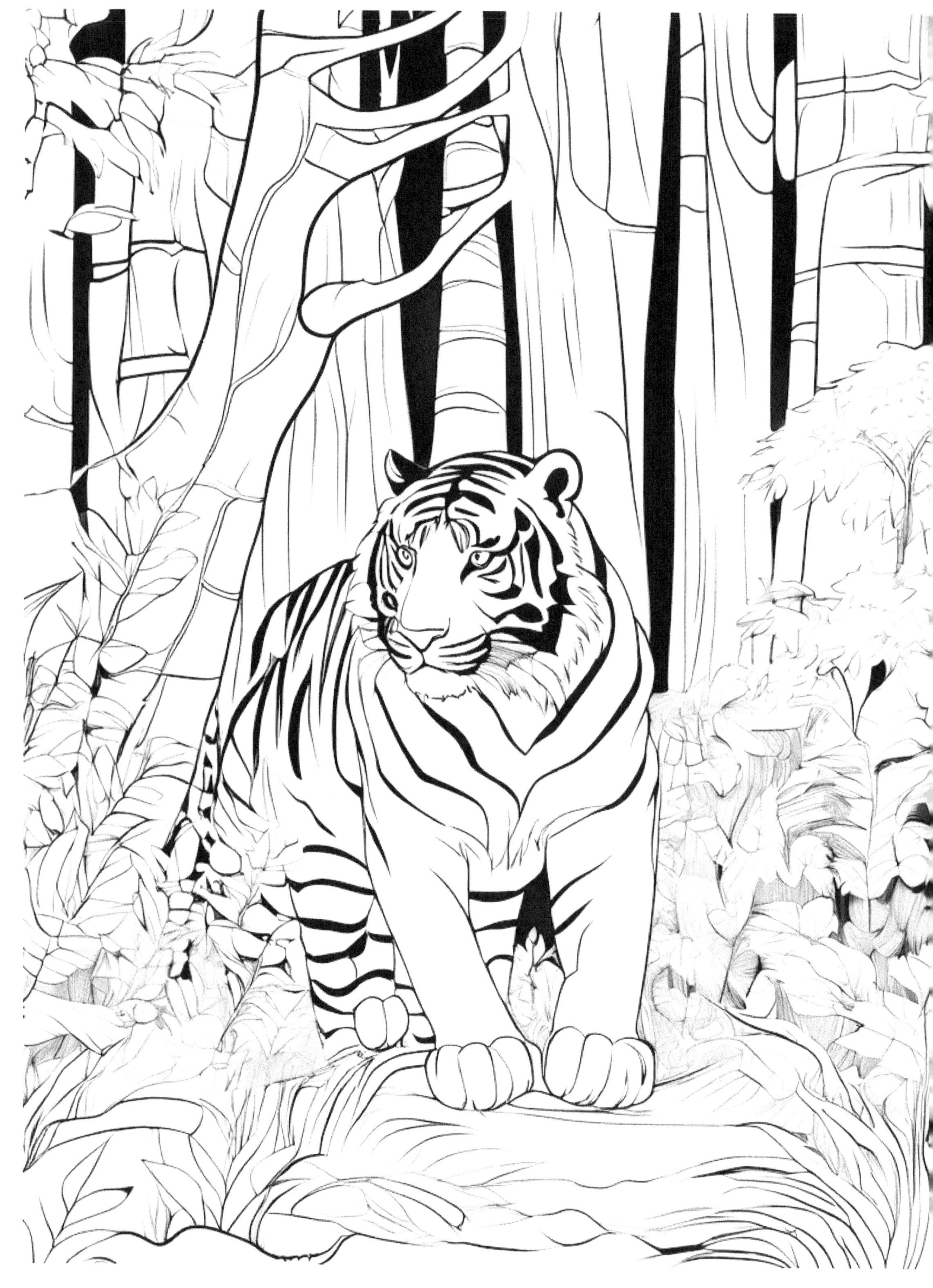

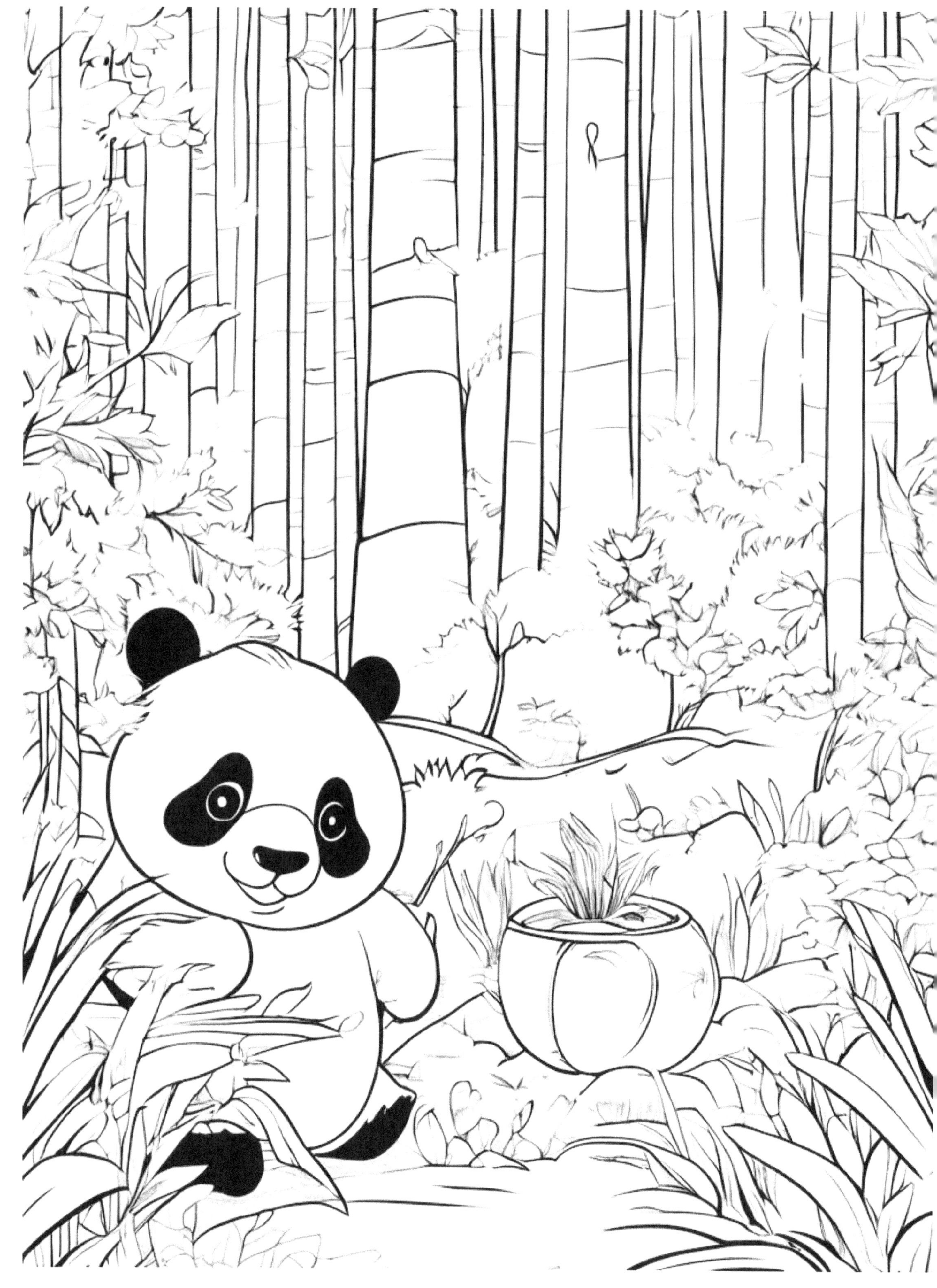

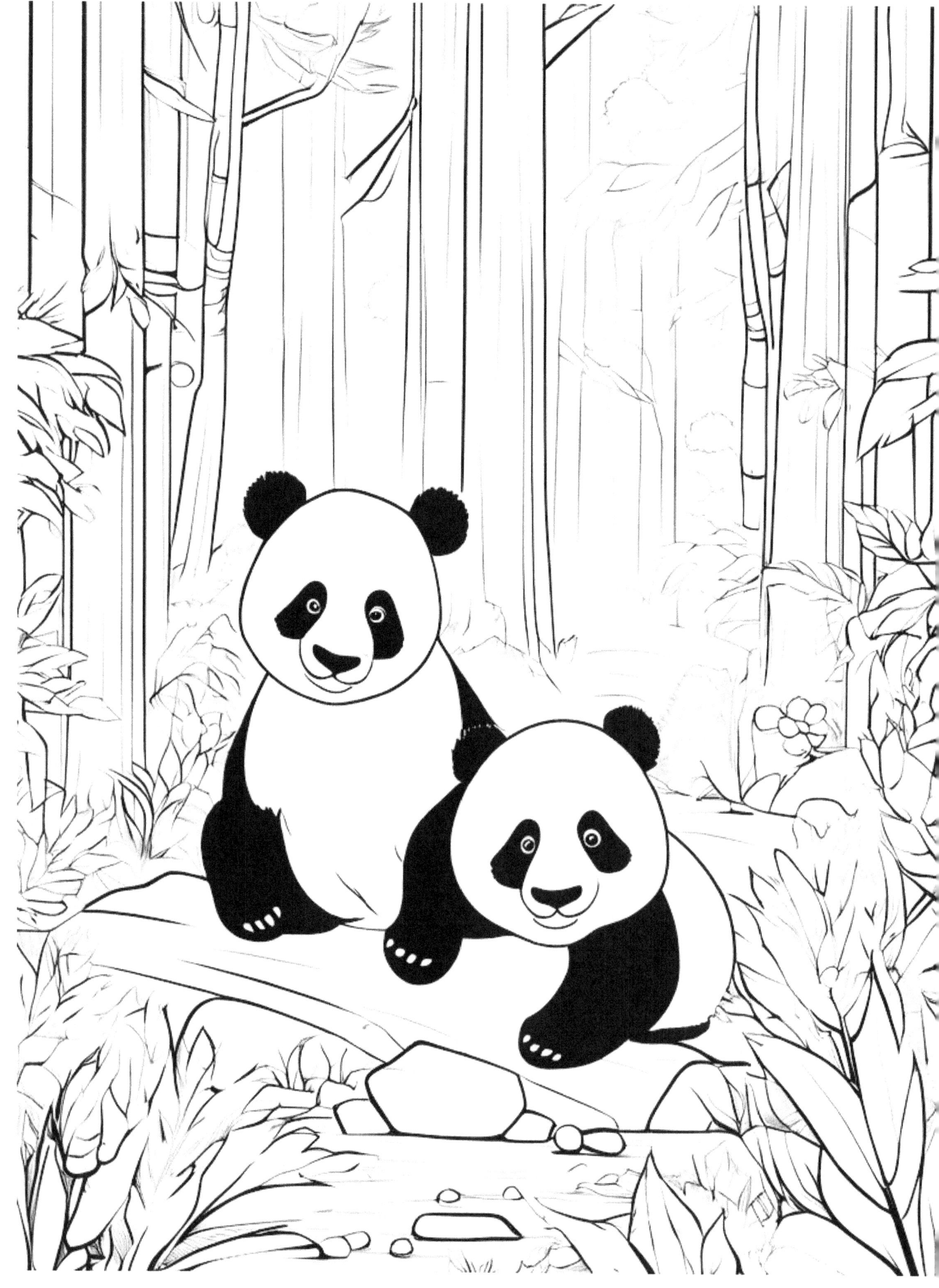

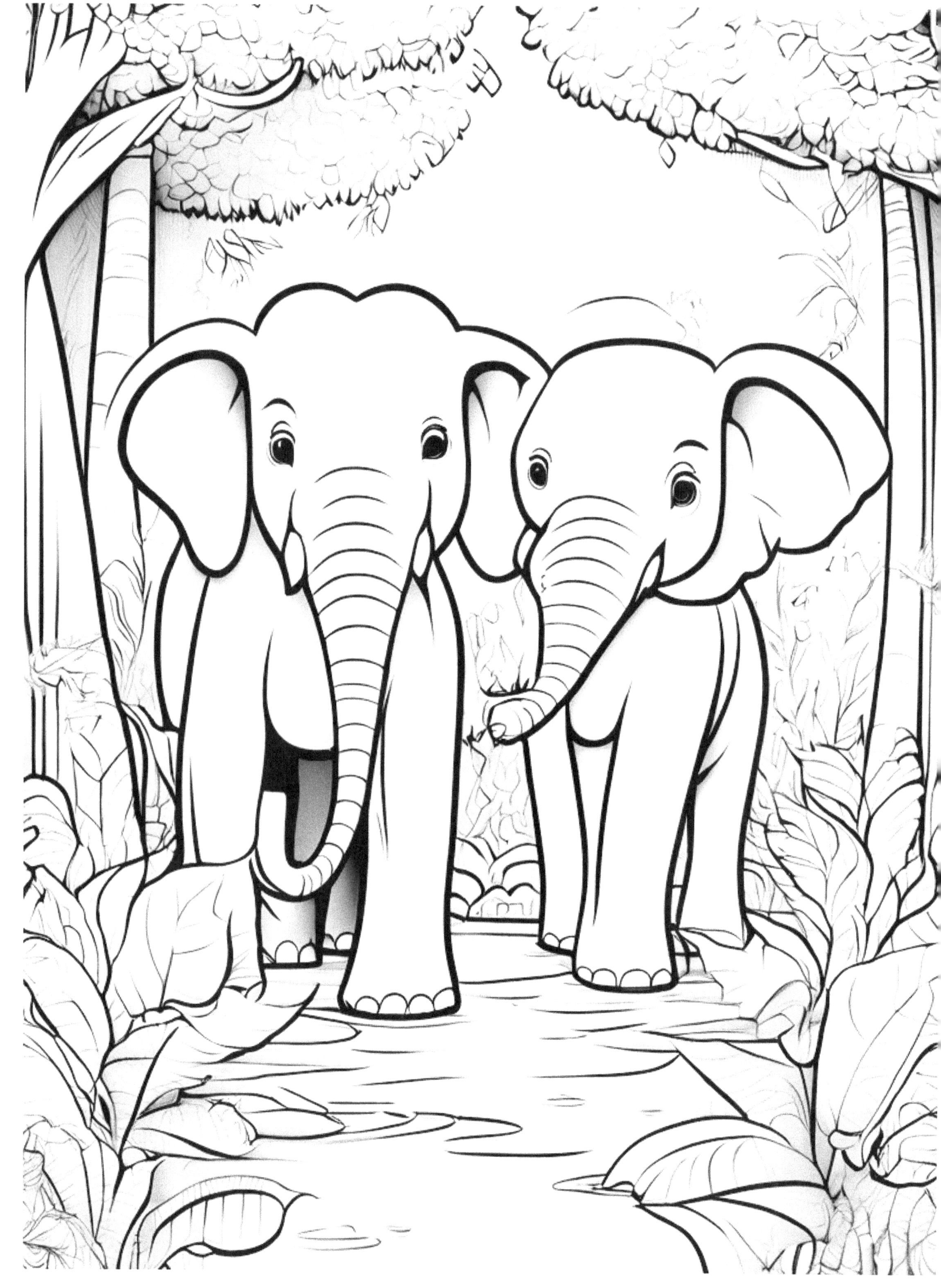

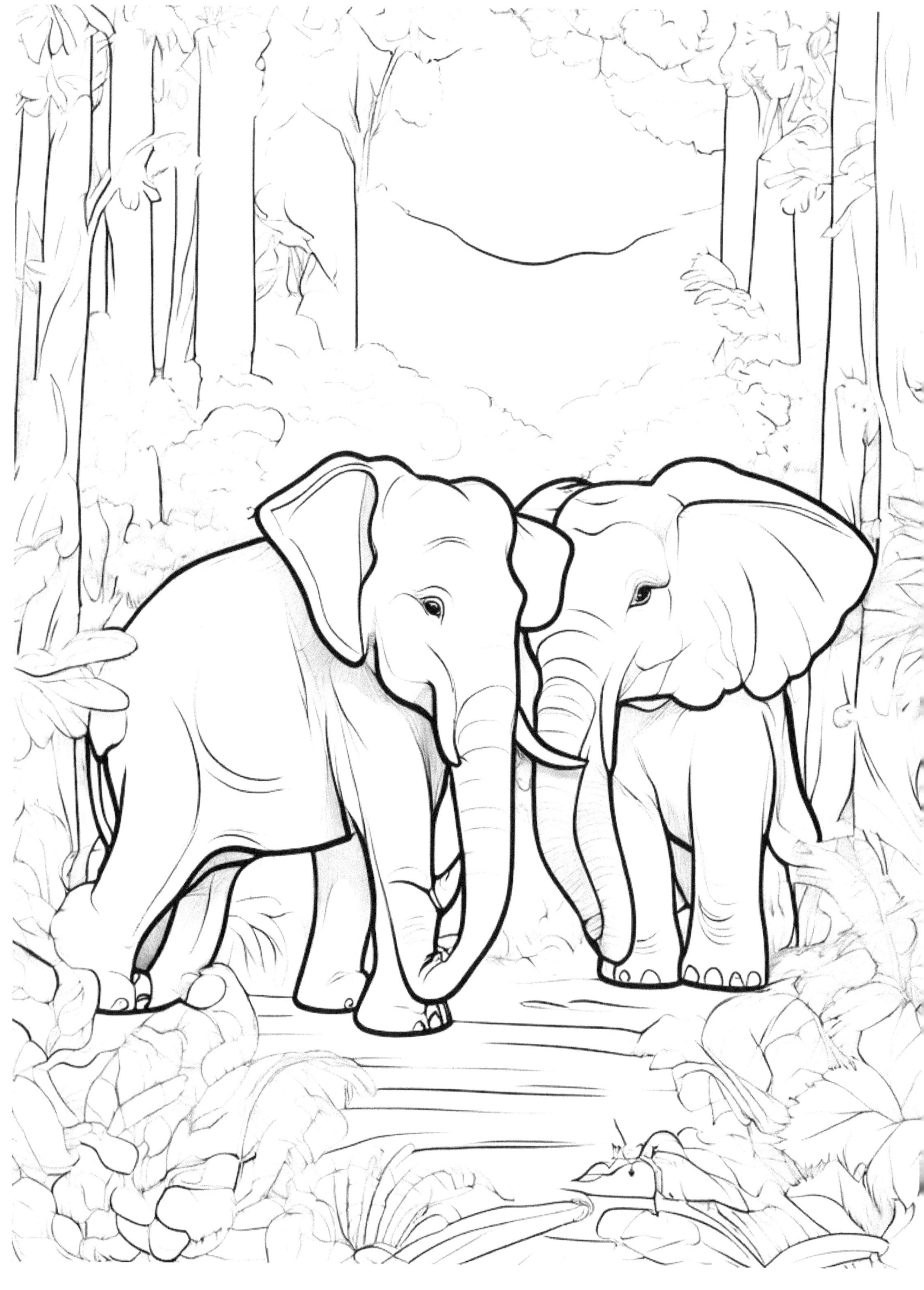

Europe:

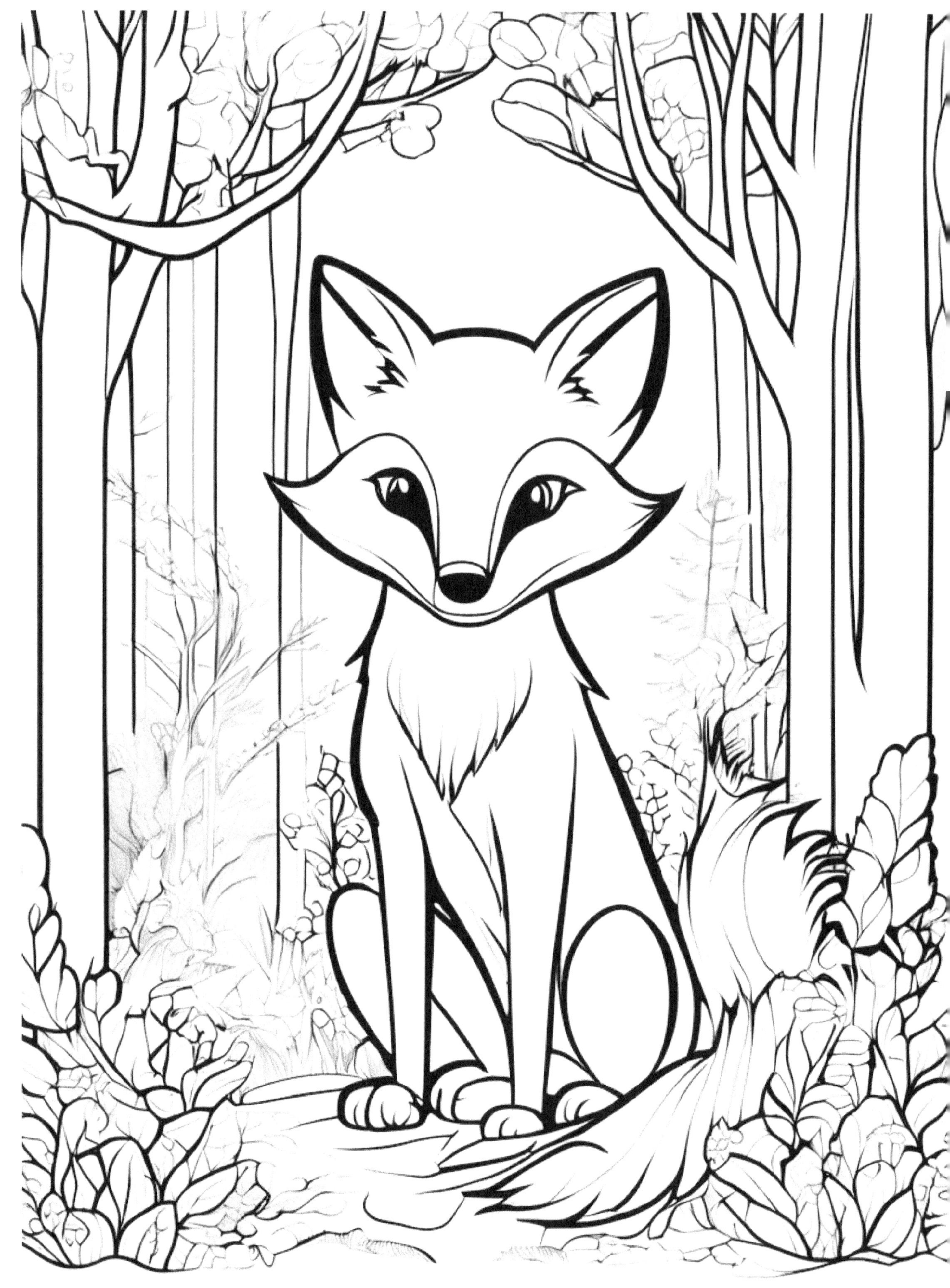

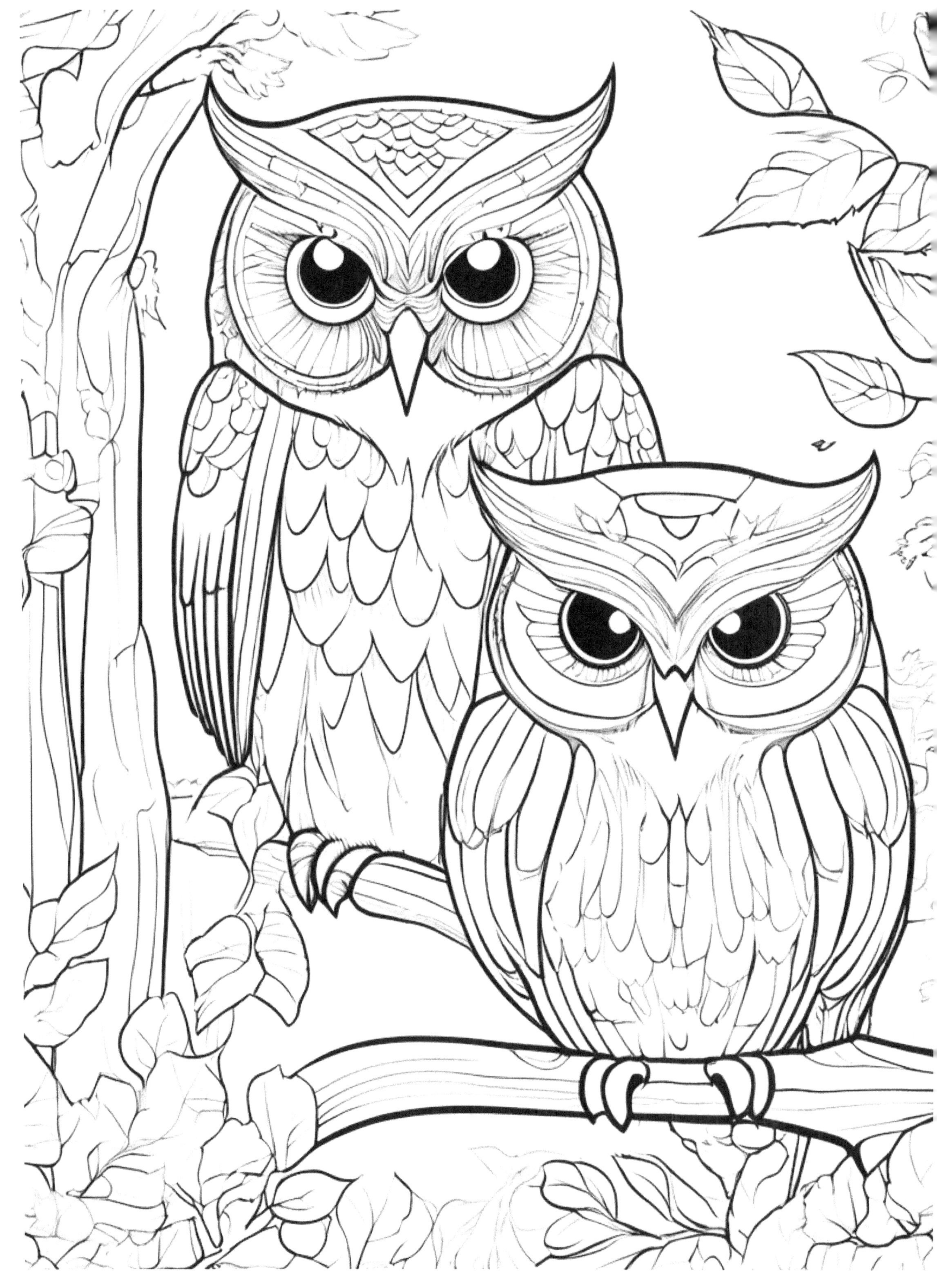

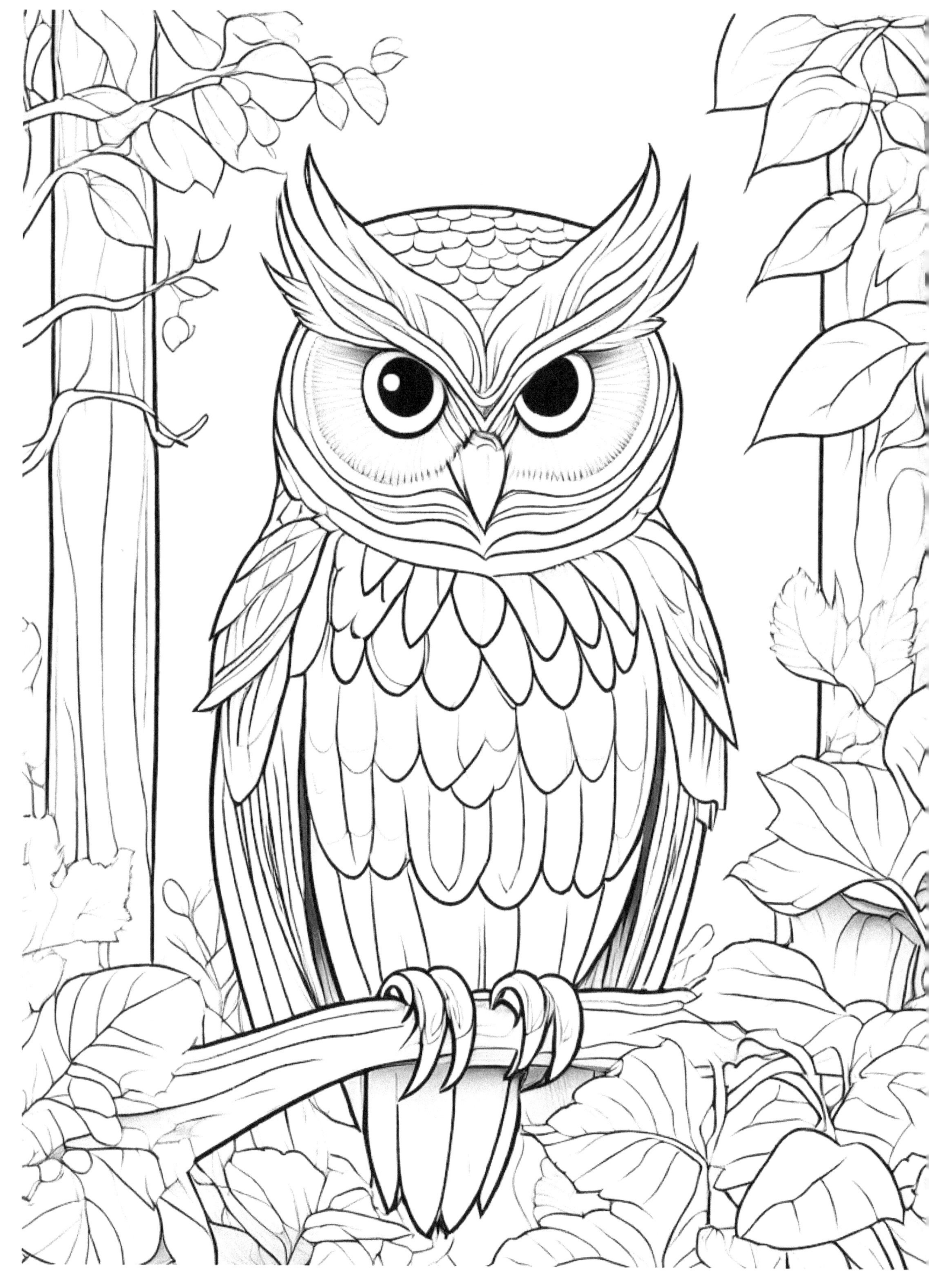

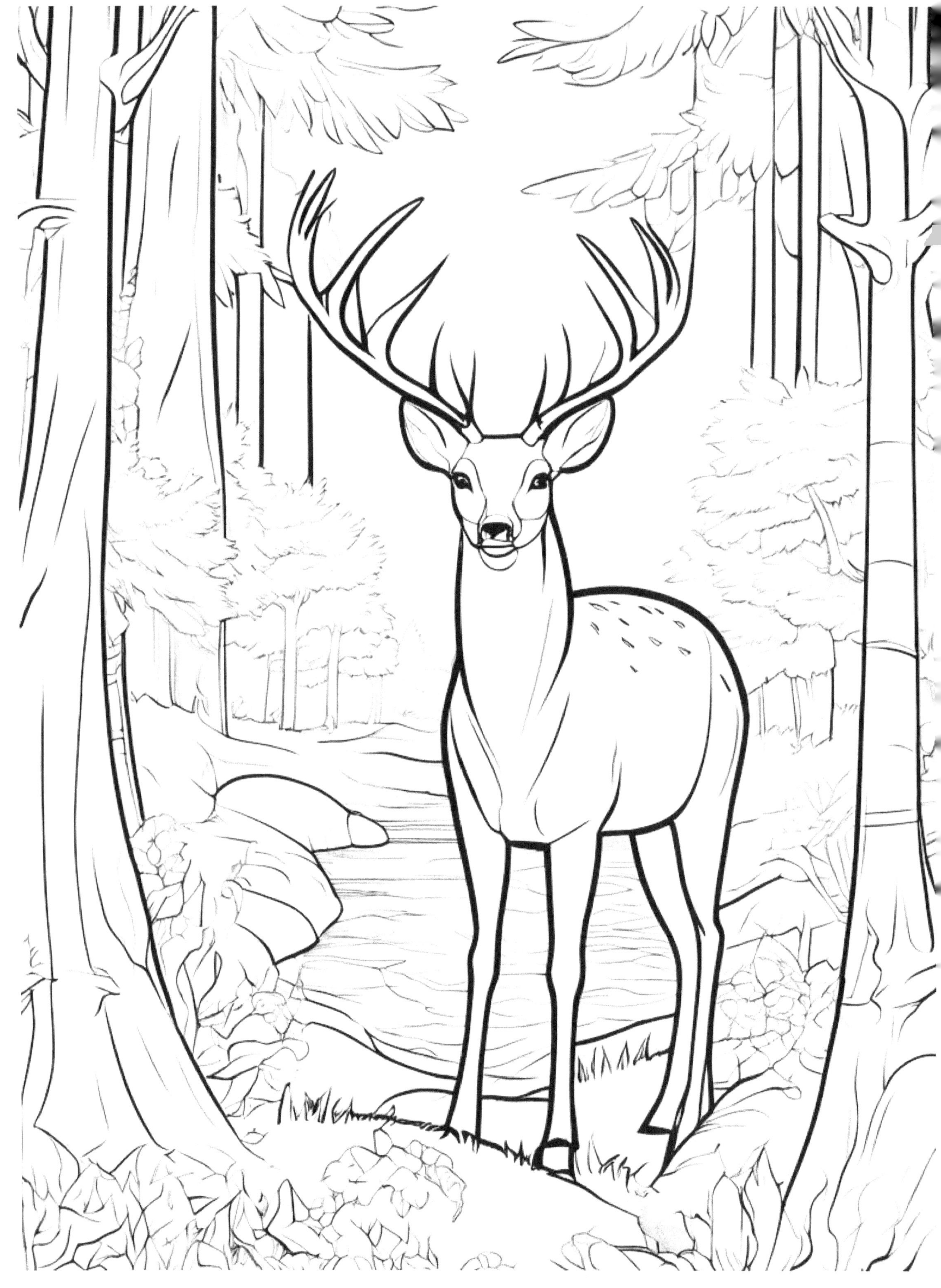

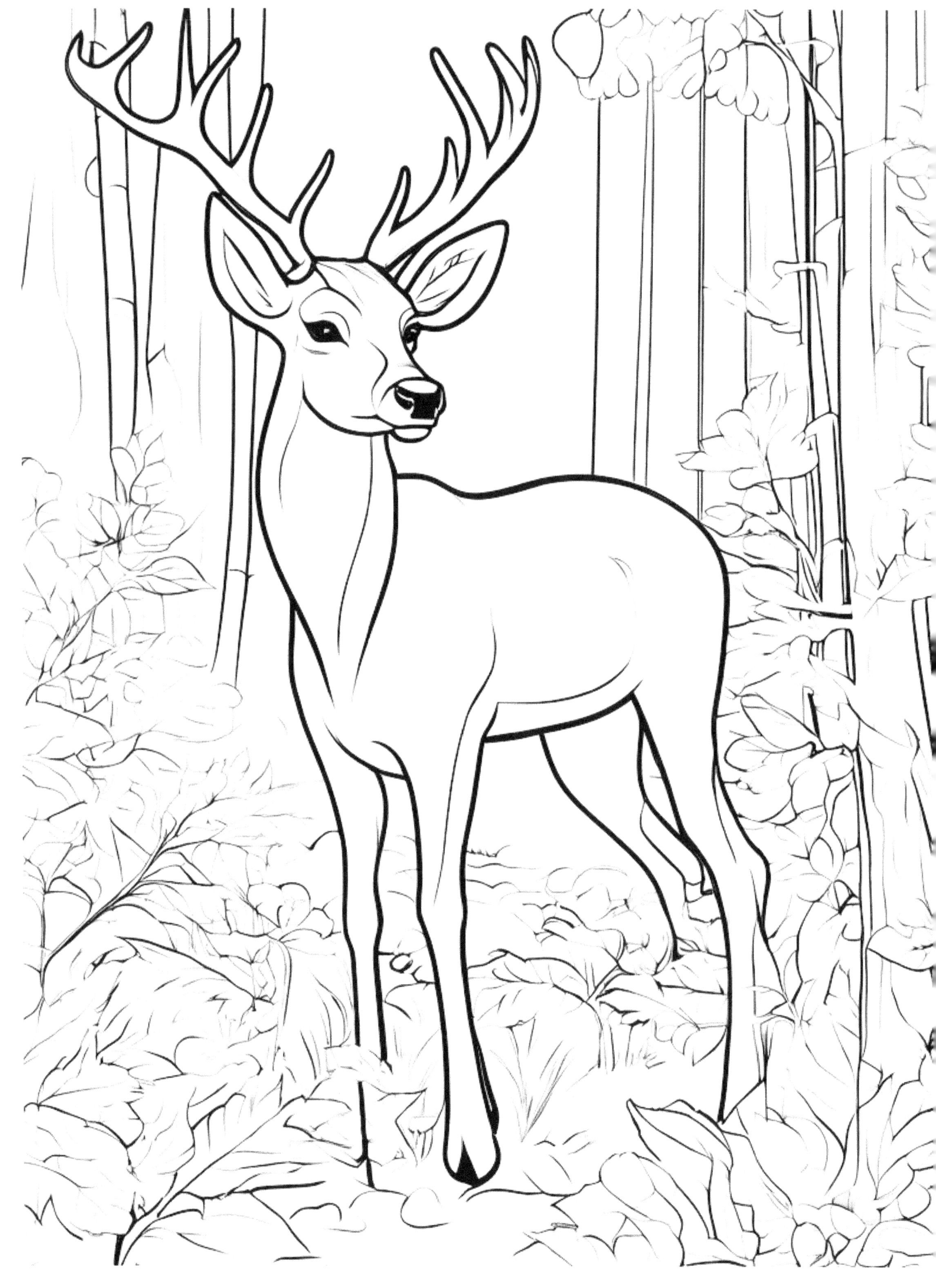

Oceania:

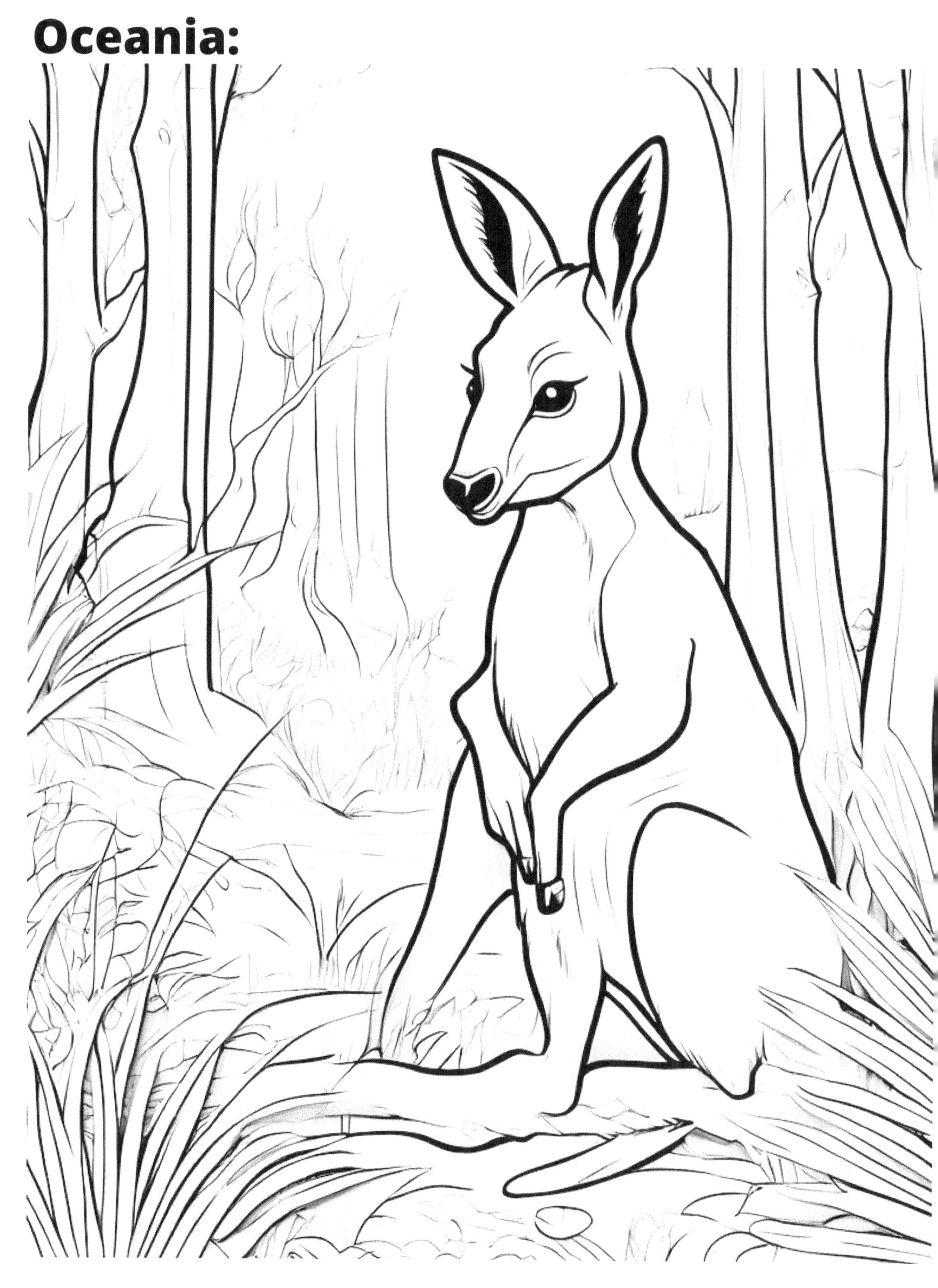

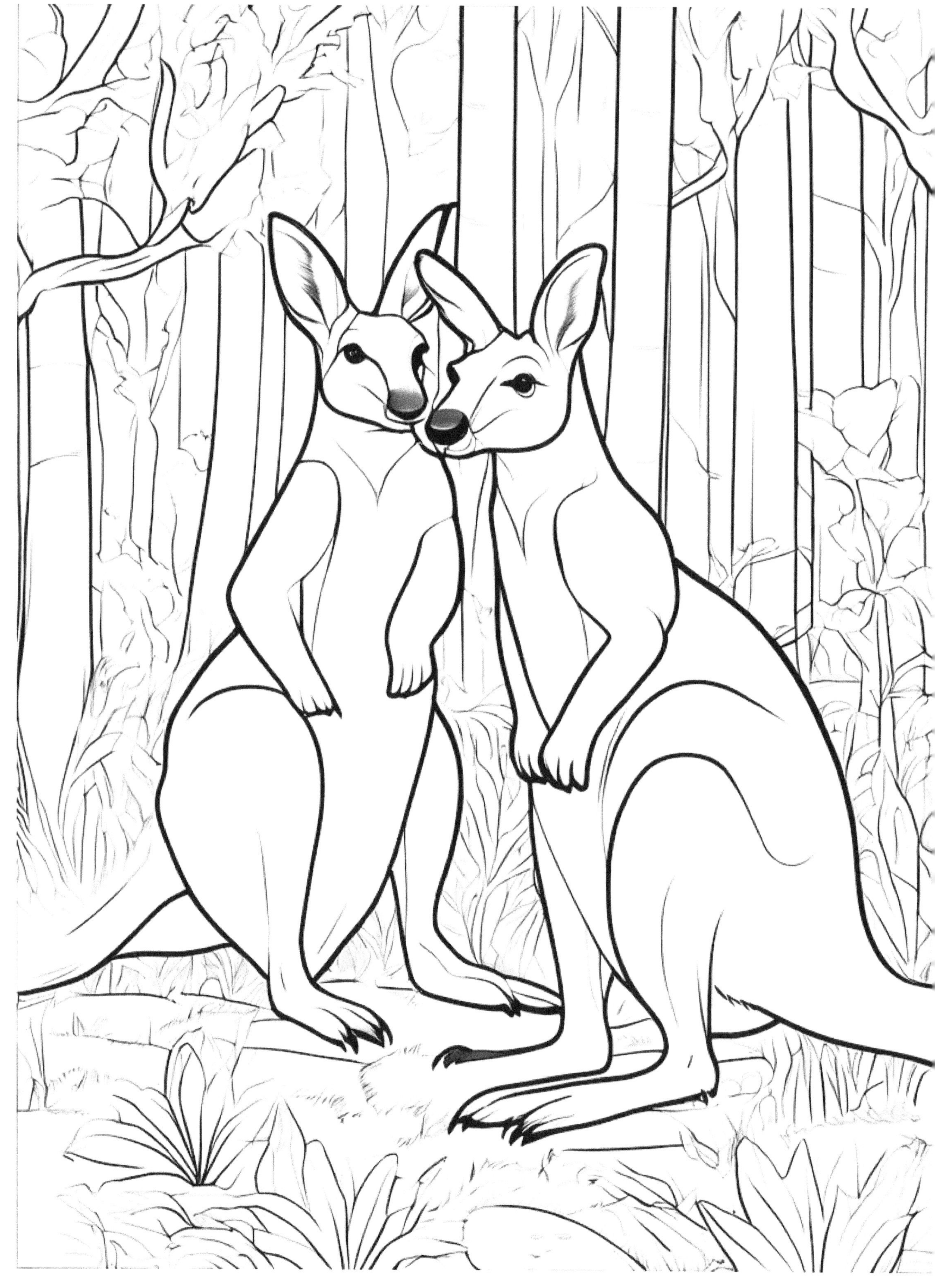

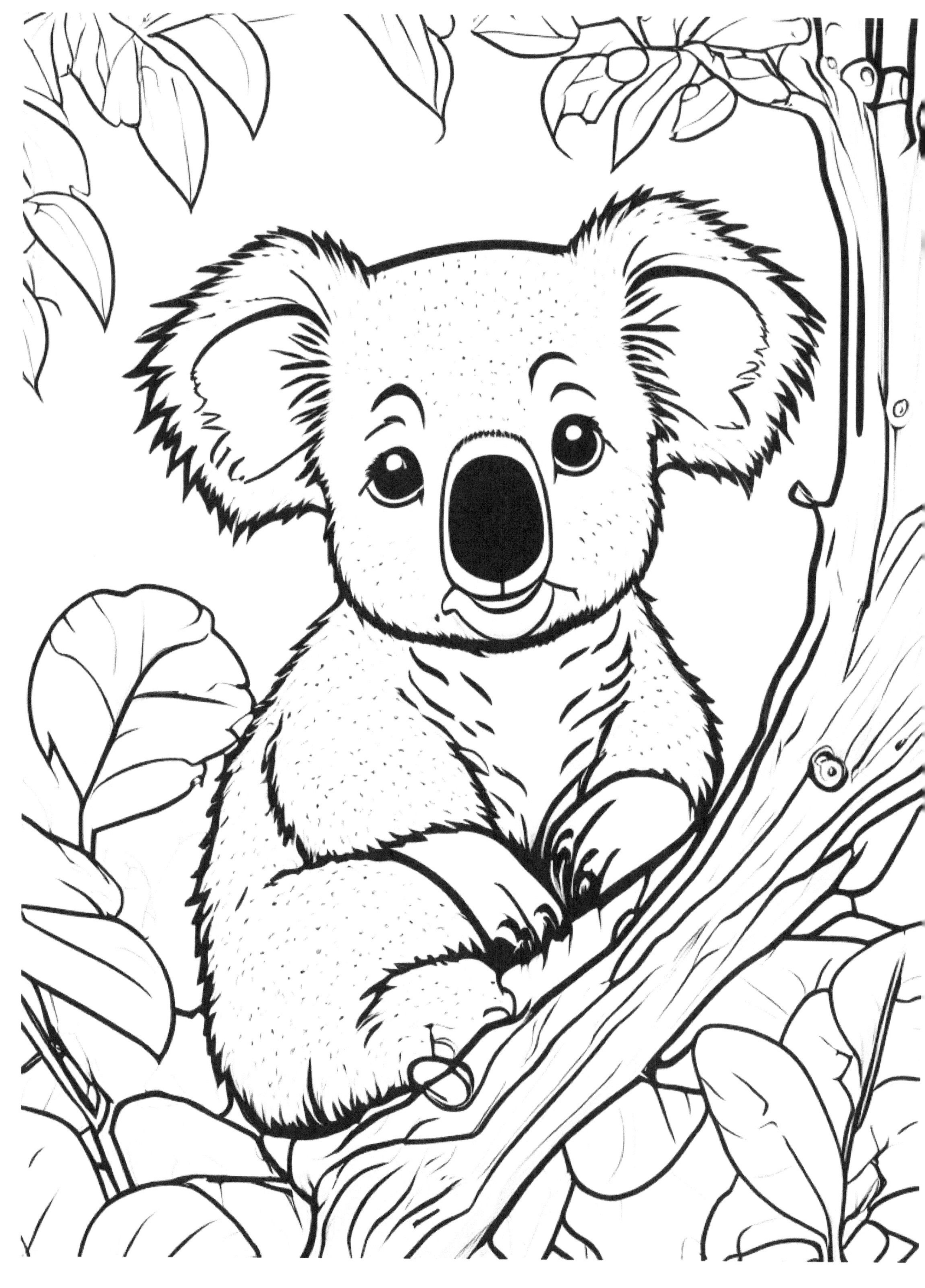

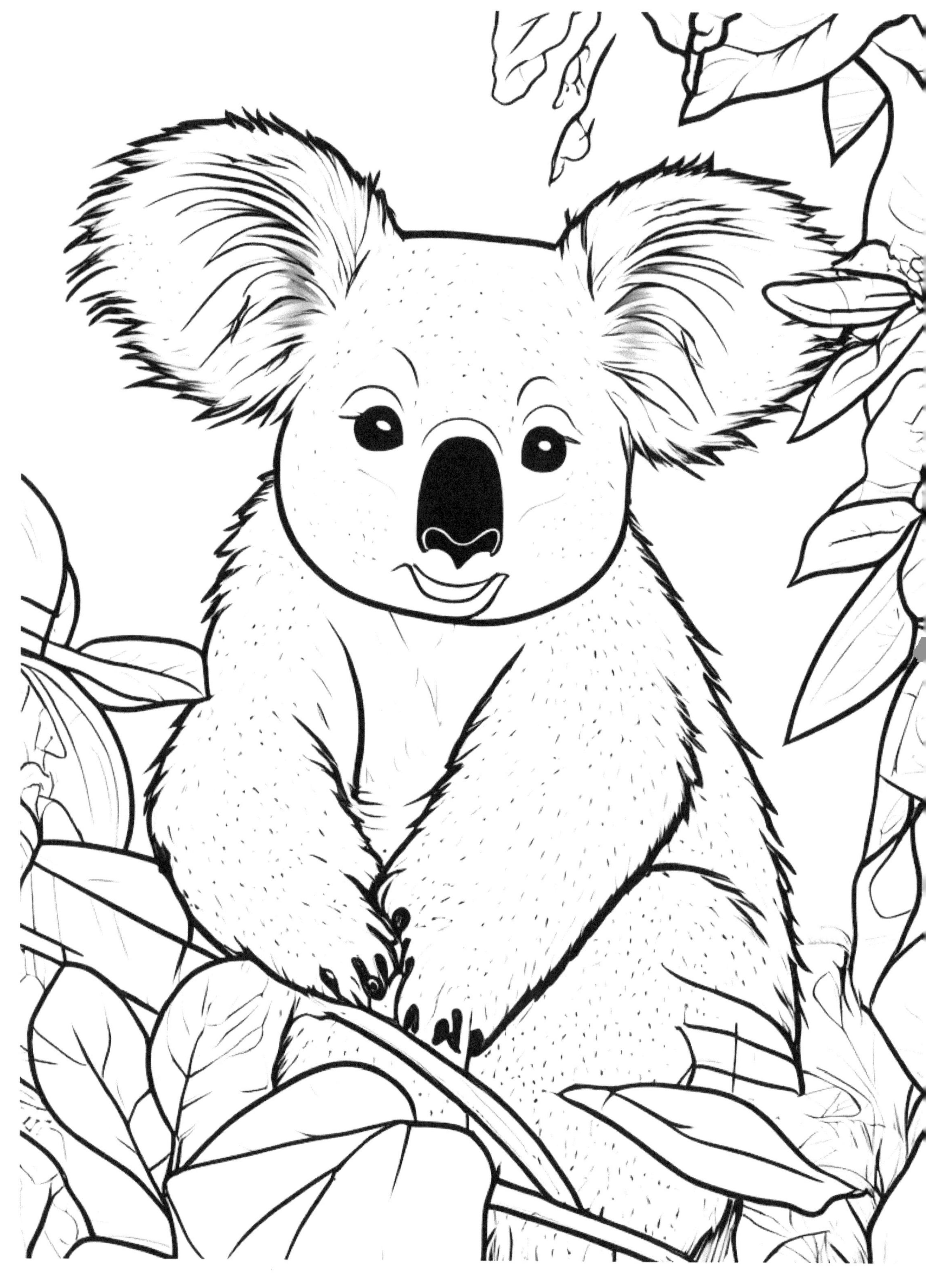

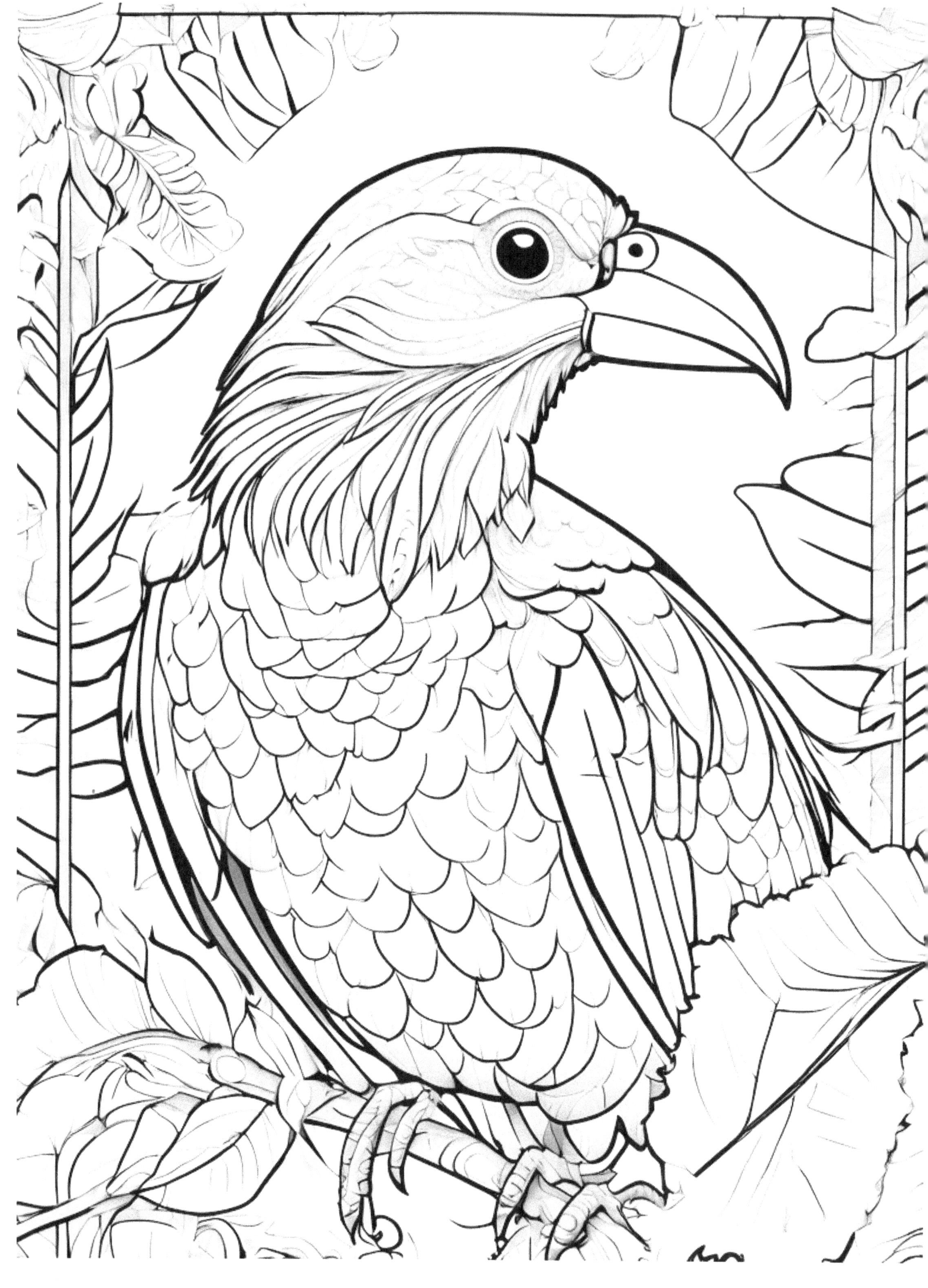

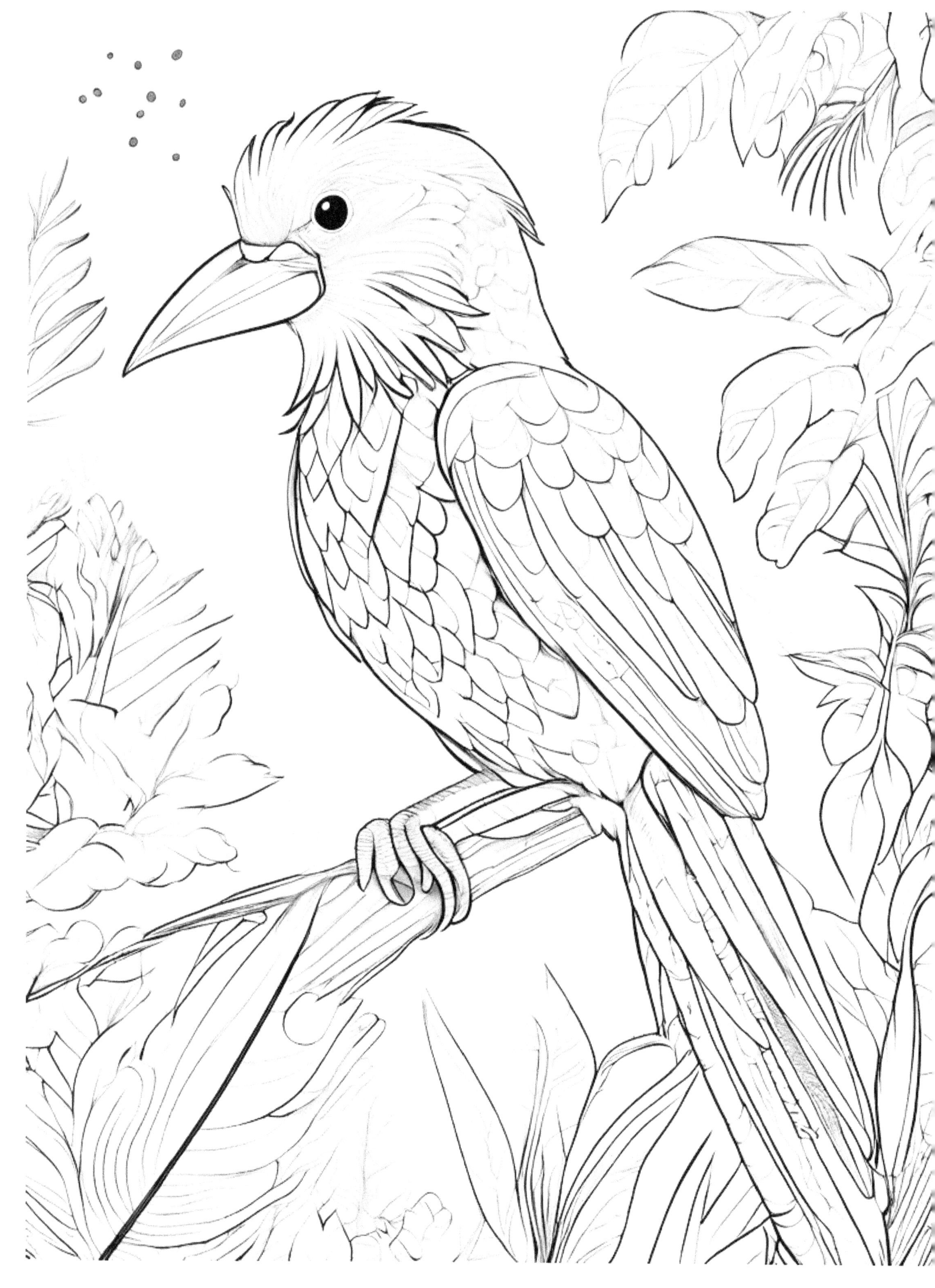

Antarctica:

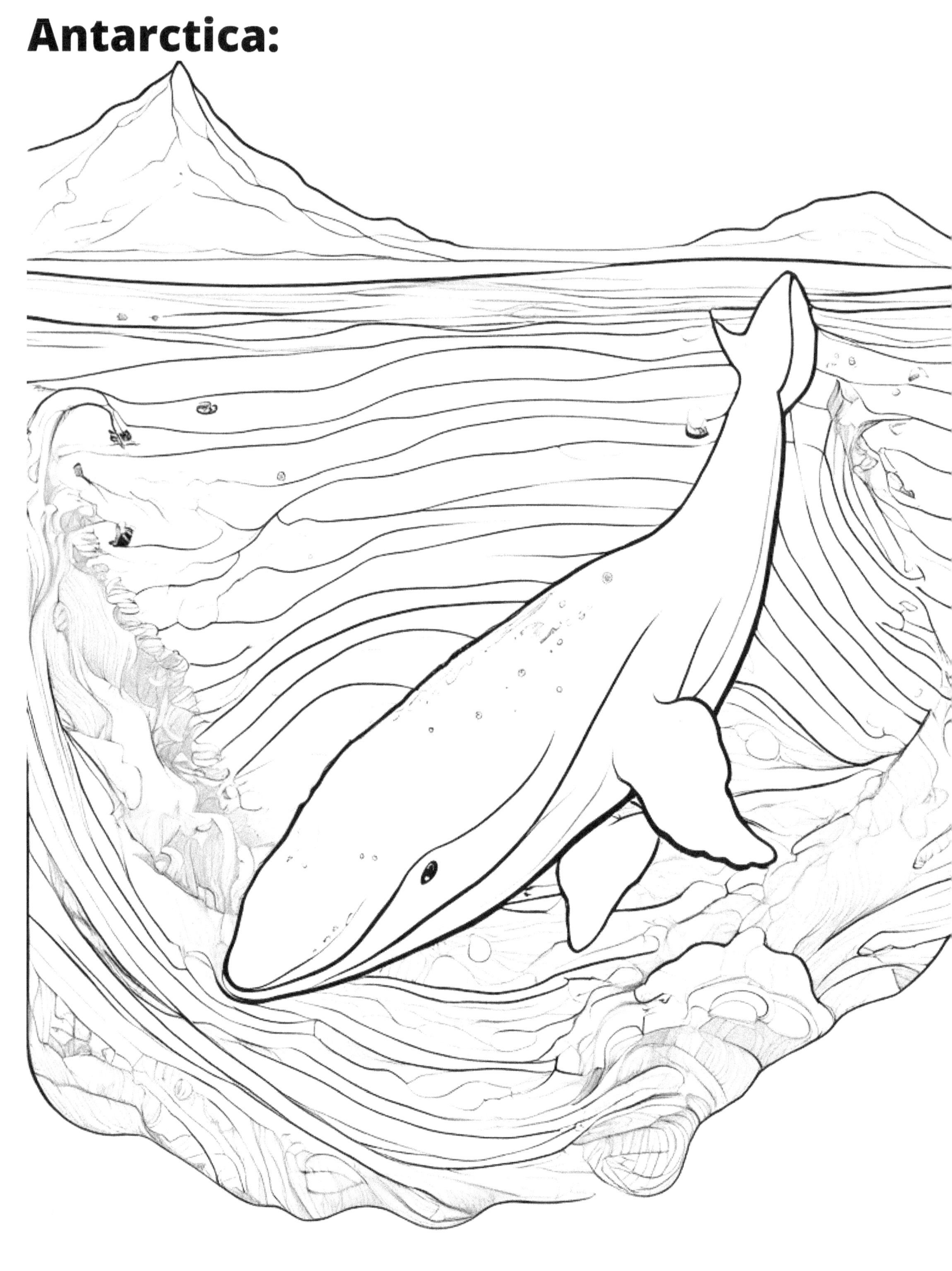

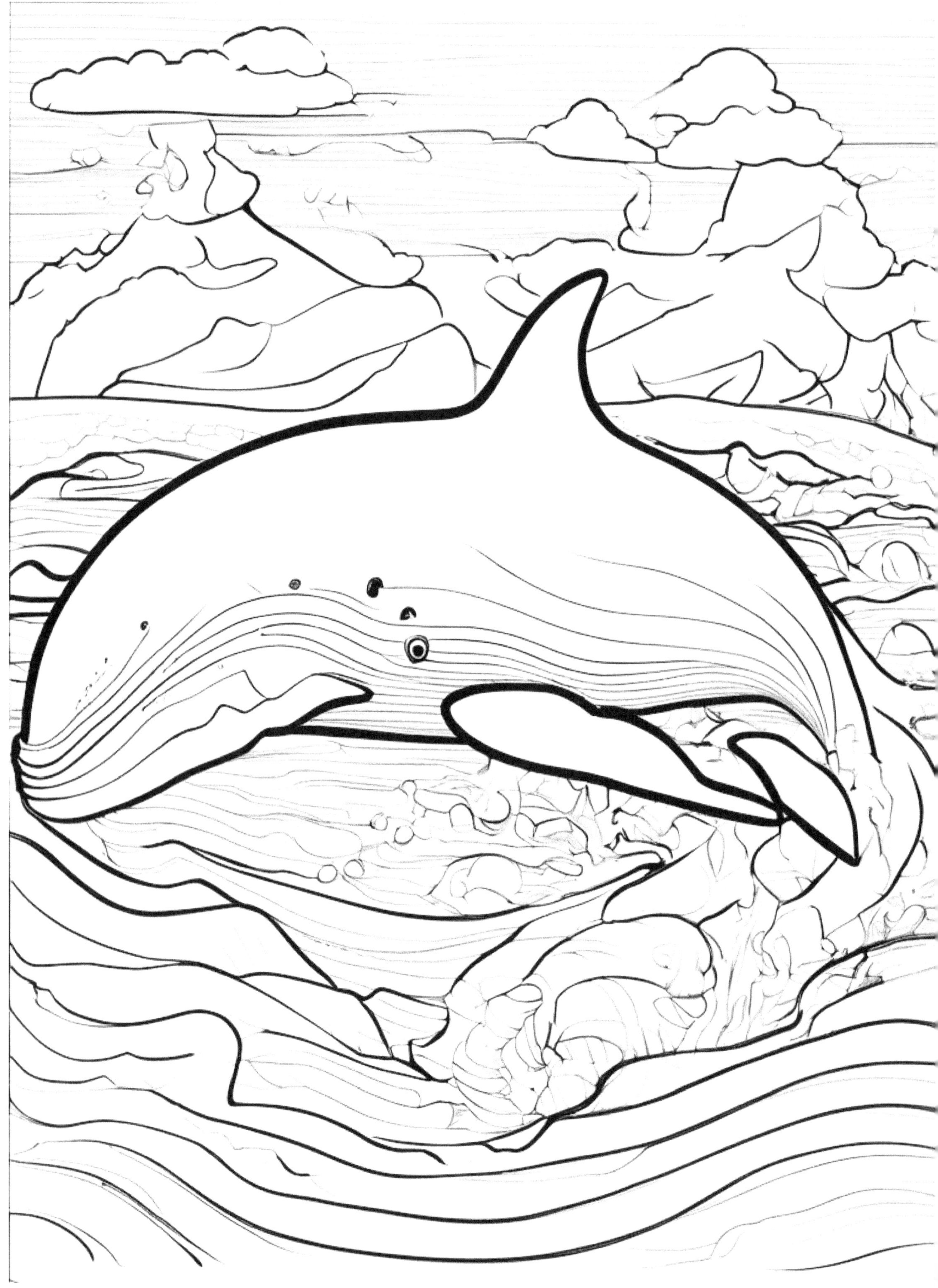

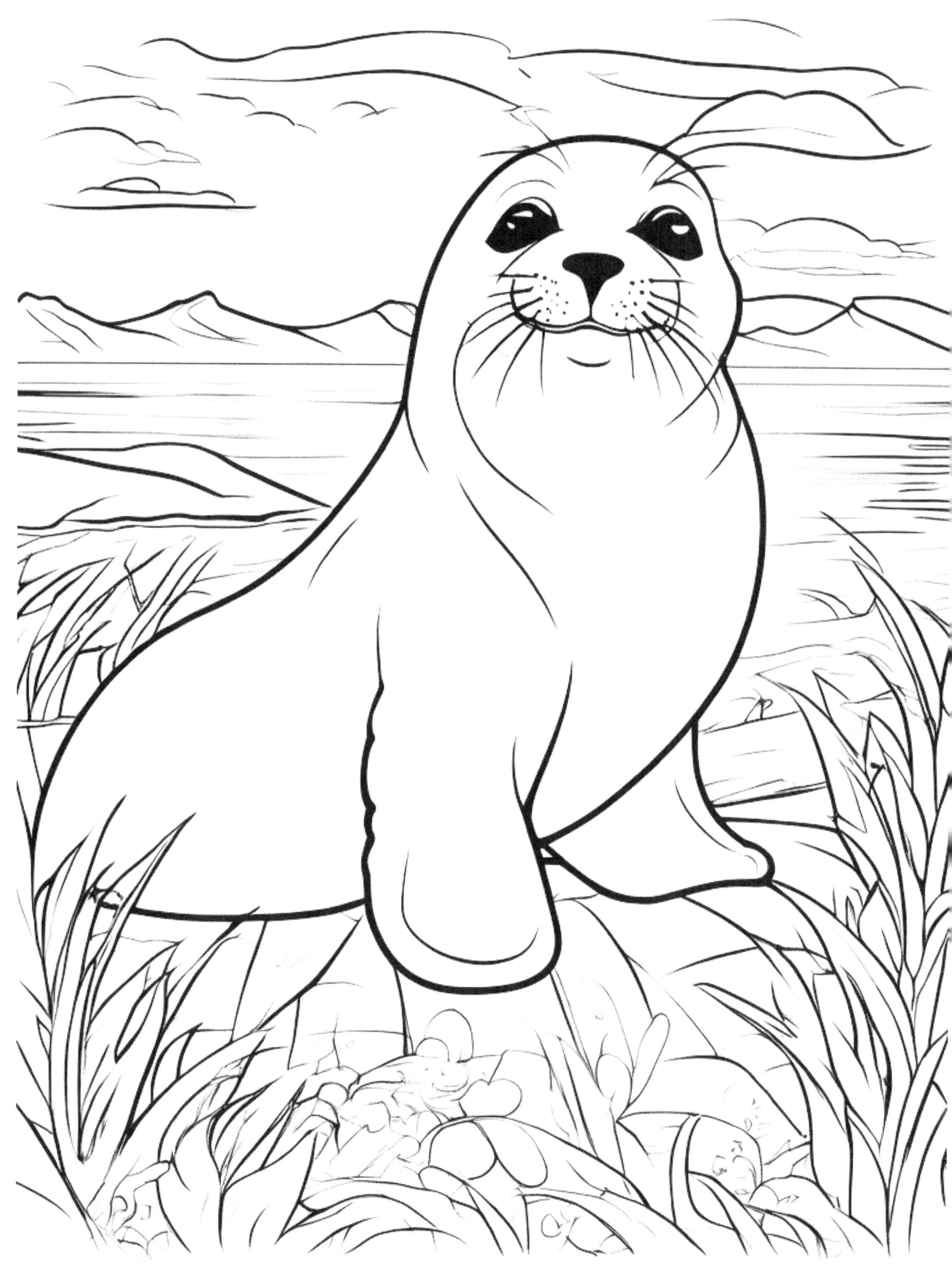

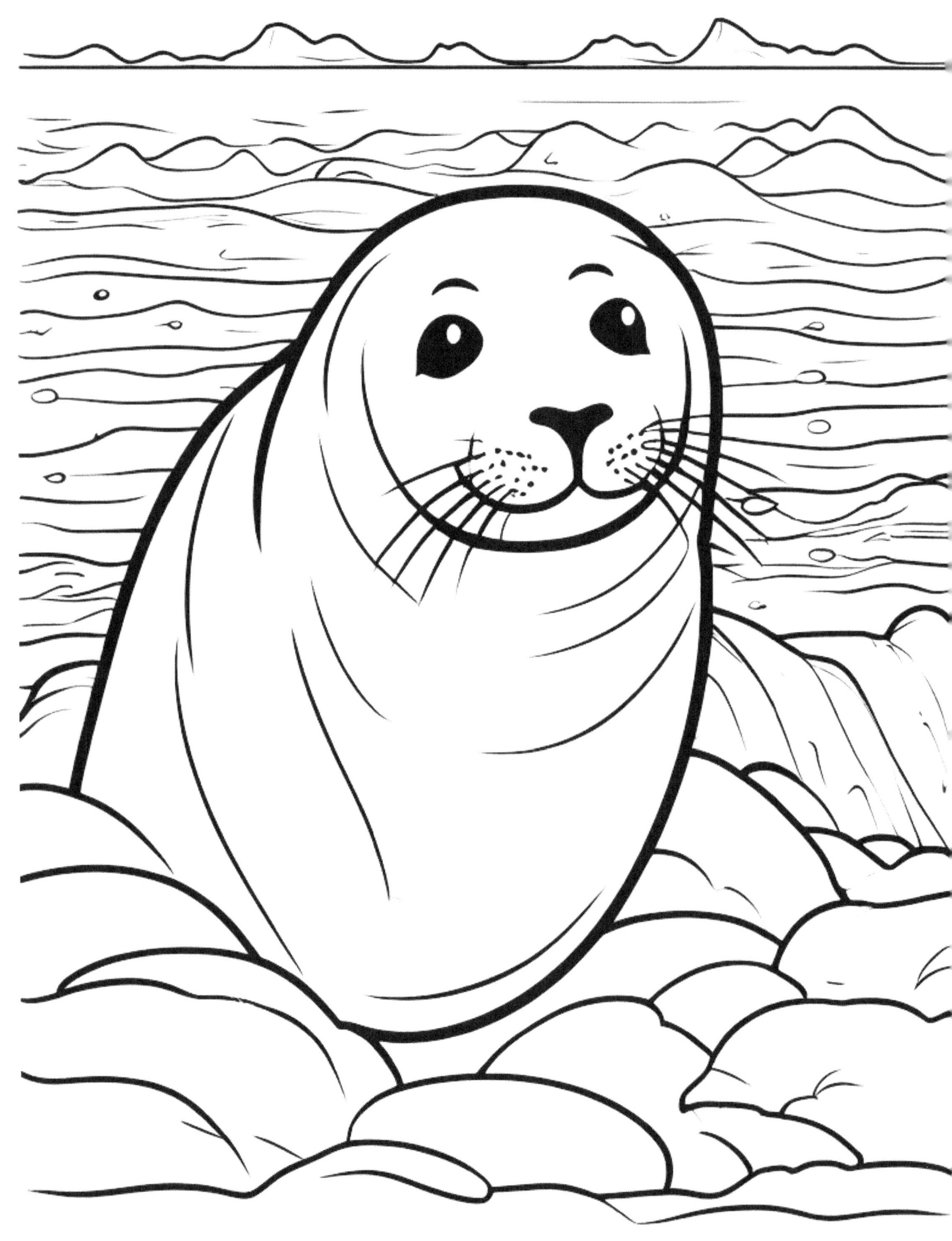

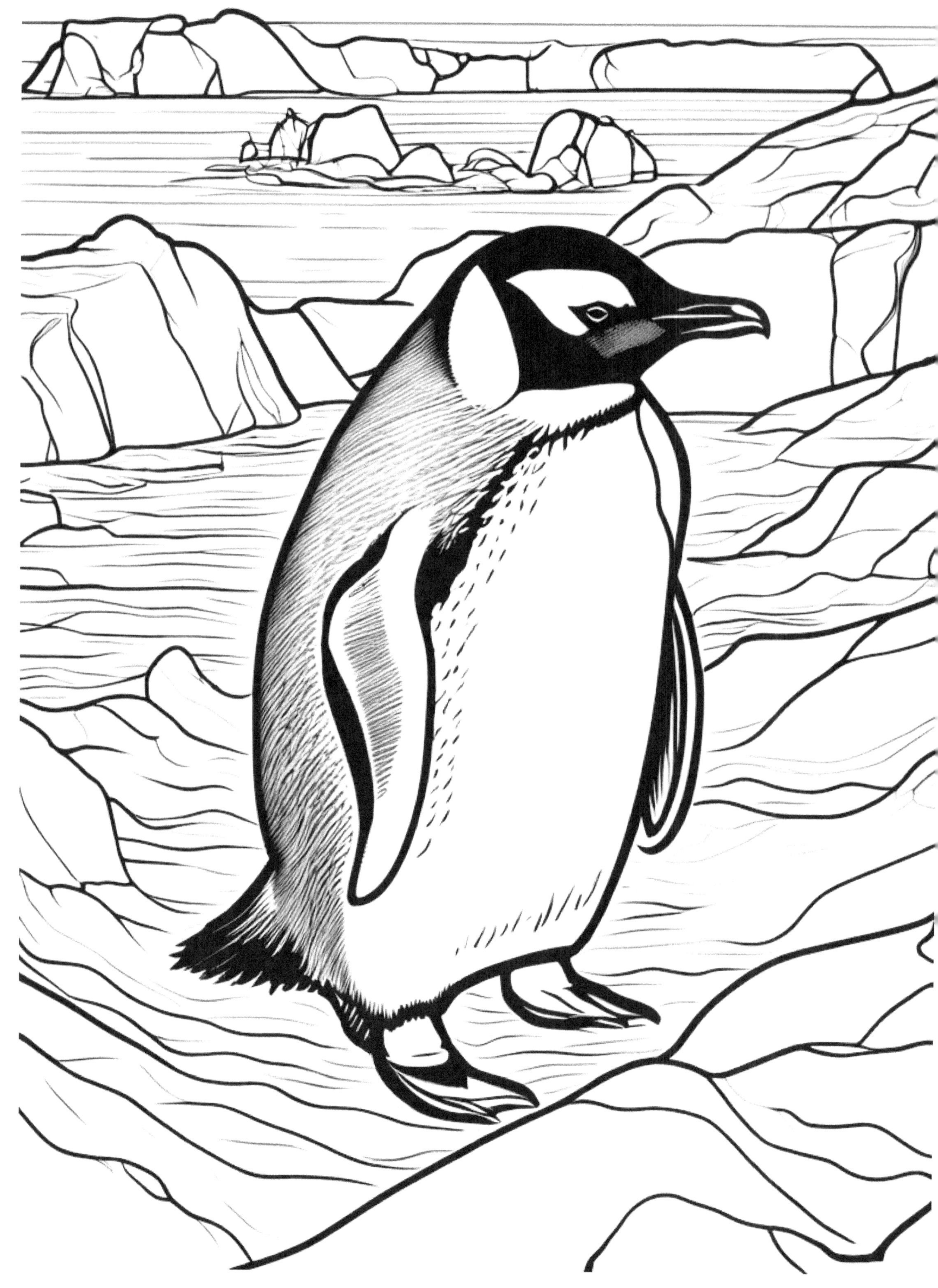

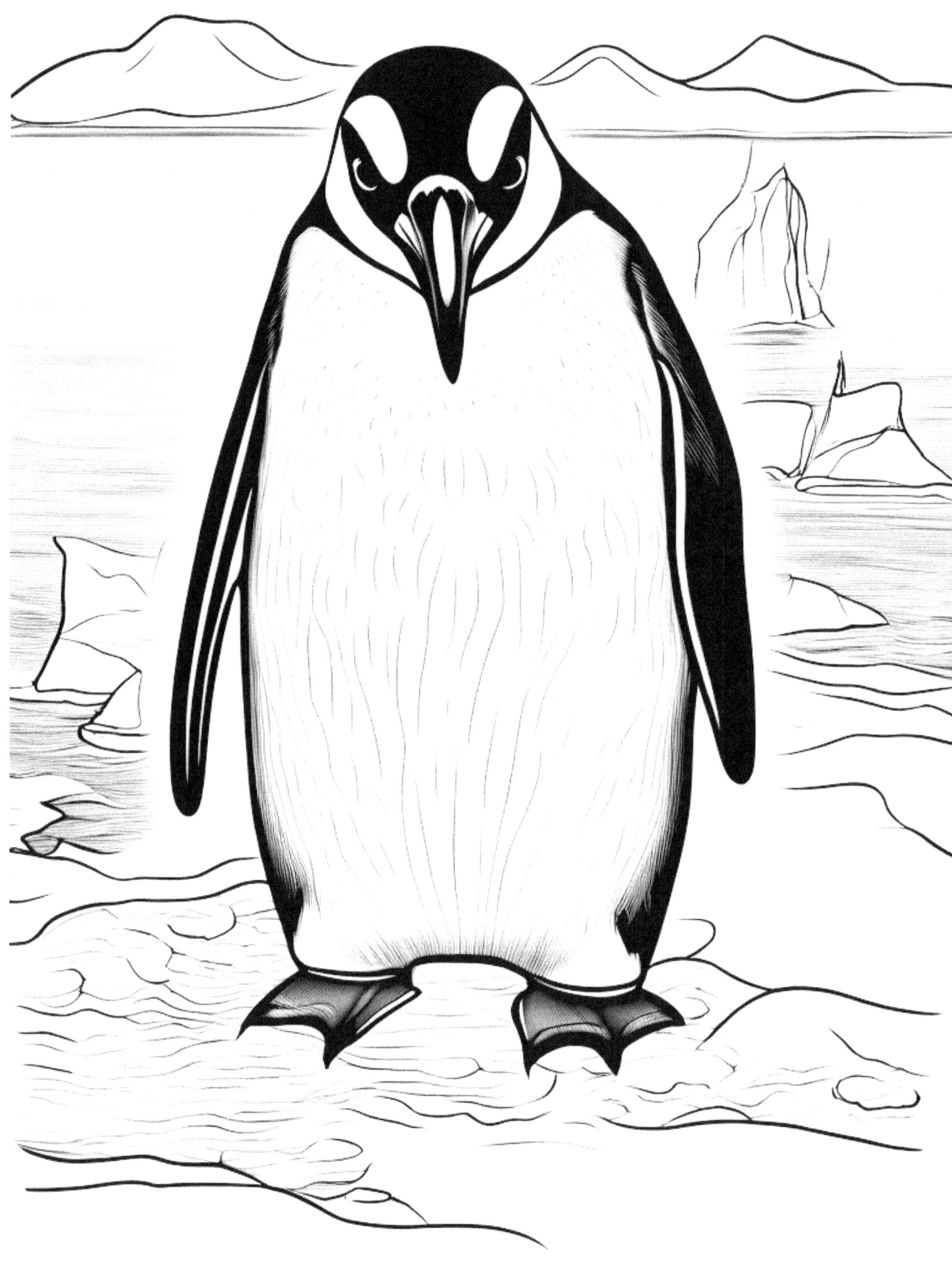